On the Other Side of Love

A woman's unconventional journey
towards wisdom

On the Other Side of Love

A woman's unconventional journey towards wisdom

Muriel Maufroy

BOOKS

Winchester, UK
Washington, USA

First published by O-Books, 2016
O-Books is an imprint of John Hunt Publishing Ltd., Laurel House, Station Approach,
Alresford, Hants, SO24 9JH, UK
office1@jhpbooks.net
www.johnhuntpublishing.com

For distributor details and how to order please visit the 'Ordering' section on our website.

Text copyright: Muriel Maufroy 2015

ISBN: 978 1 78535 281 2
Library of Congress Control Number: 2015949729

A CIP catalogue record for this book is available from the British Library.

Design: Stuart Davies

Printed and bound by CPI Group (UK) Ltd, Croydon, CR0 4YY, UK

We operate a distinctive and ethical publishing philosophy in all
areas of our business, from our global network of authors to
production and worldwide distribution.

CONTENTS

By the same author

Breathing Truth
Rumi's Daughter
The Garden of Hafez

To all those who have guided my steps along the way, especially Jean Gibson and Gedaliah Fleer, whose generosity and wisdom changed everything.

You must destroy the house in order to find the treasure hidden under it.
– Jalaluddin Rumi

Paris 2014

The cardboard box stored on the shelf of the cupboard had remained unopened for years. It had followed her in her moves – three of them – the latest from London to Paris, each time without her ever having the inclination to look into it. She thought it was full of books, the kind of books one keeps out of loyalty to the past, even though the desire to read them has long gone.

That day though, she was determined to empty the box and give the books away. But when she opened it, to her surprise, there were no books there. Instead was a pile of concert programmes and under it, a large green folder she immediately recognized; it contained a part of her past she had for years kept at a safe distance. Inside were the notes she'd written in Israel some twenty years ago, her correspondence with RezaLeah, with Ka-Tzetnik, the tapes of interviews she had made during that same period. The notes covered no more than a few dozen pages, but they carried the same intensity that had permeated her life at the time: the abyss of despair she had fallen into, the powerful encounters, some apparently accidental, that had taken place. It was hardly a decision; it was imperative: She had to look again and try to reconstruct a past that for two decades she had left untouched.

But as the past began to unfold, it became increasingly obvious that the person that emerged was very different from the one she was today. There, was Marie struggling with her life and here she was, looking at herself with a mixture of astonishment, compassion and new understanding.

Falling Apart

Jerusalem – May 1994

The drive through the hills seemed to last forever. Neither of them spoke. Where was he taking her? They had no house to go to, no room, no bed. She should have been afraid; instead, she felt numb, indifferent to her fate. She didn't know and didn't want to know his name, nor had he asked hers. He was just a young taxi driver, the same who had driven her through Jerusalem the previous day. They had agreed to meet at night in front of the convent, the one she had spent her first two nights in, and now he was in charge.

When he finally stopped the car, she saw that they had reached a small ledge overlooking the city. Lights flickered in the distance: a place where, on weekends, people perhaps came for a picnic, though there was nowhere to sit or lie down here. As far as she could see, the ground under her feet was dry, dusty and covered with stones.

He was standing facing her. Marie had her back to the car. Around them, the dark silence of the night. He pushed her against the car, pulled at her skirt, undid his belt, pulled down her underwear and forced himself into her, violently, brutally. She closed her eyes. This was rape, but she the 'victim' was no victim. This was an act she had willed, an act of self-destruction, the way to clear herself of Alex's imprint, the way to erase him. Some might have called it a death wish. Well, to live or to die, what was the difference?

It was quickly over and they both got into the car, neither of them uttering a word. What was there to say? He handed her a piece of cloth to wipe herself. There was blood on the cloth. Sacrificial blood, she thought. Something had been accomplished; she was not quite sure what, and putting it into words was impossible. She kept at a distance his tangible contempt.

What had happened had nothing to do with him. She had used him as he had used her: to him she was an outlet for his sexual frustration; to her this was an exorcism that might set her free from Alex.

He dropped her at the gate of the Convent of the Poor Clares where she was staying, an oasis of quietness and purity she hoped her presence would not soil. They, of course, never saw each other again.

Jerusalem – May 1994 – Gedaliah

She walked up the four steps leading to Gedaliah's door and rang the bell. 'If you ever come to Jerusalem,' the rabbi had said that last time in California, 'you must come and visit me.' When was that? Two, three years ago? Time didn't make sense anymore. All she knew was that it was before Alex. Marie remembered thinking at the time that there was little chance she would ever set foot in Israel, but she didn't want to embarrass Gedaliah and she carefully wrote his details in the small address book she kept in her bag, the one she hardly ever consulted. And yet, here she was, wondering what exactly she was going to tell him.

She glanced back at the square behind her. From the top of the steps, it looked like the stage of a theatre with the small café and its tables and chairs set on one side, and in the far corner, the jacaranda that extended its purple blossoms over a group of small children arguing loudly. Among them, a small girl, five years old at the most, her red hair parted in plaits, a miniature version of RezaLeah. Had time gone backward and was she watching the child RezaLeah of fifty years ago? Marie brushed the thought away. Two men with side curls, white shirts loosely tucked into black trousers, were hurrying towards the coolness of a lane where they disappeared as if swallowed by some giant maw. The country was in the grip of a heatwave and the sun, now at its zenith, was beating the city. 'Quite unusual at this time of year,' people kept saying. Marie certainly had not expected such sweltering heat in May. But what did it matter? Nothing mattered, even her standing here, feeling like an empty shell, unable to think further than this very moment. It crossed her mind that she was one of the actors on the stage, cast in a play that held no meaning for her, even though she couldn't leave the stage and escape from the pain that, worse than the heat, gripped her heart.

The door in front of her finally opened. There stood the same large man with kind eyes she remembered from their last meeting. Without warning and before she could say anything, tears broke out. 'Come in,' he said with a welcome gesture of the hand, apparently unfazed by her tears. 'How long are you staying in Jerusalem?' he asked once they sat face to face in a small room filled with the two armchairs they were sitting in, a desk covered with papers, and a sofa on which was spread half a dozen books, some of them still open.

'Three weeks,' she said, wiping the tears with the inside of her wrist.

'That's time enough,' Gedaliah said matter-of-factly, while offering her a Kleenex. Then, as she wondered, time enough for what? he added, 'You'll come three or four times a week, and we'll work together.' She had no idea of what he meant by 'work', but acquiesced with a nod. When drowning, you do not refuse a lifebelt, even if it comes from an unexpected corner. And so, unwittingly, she began her slow climb out of the pit of darkness that, thirty days earlier, had engulfed her.

Paris 2014

An image rises up as she remembers: an abandoned house whose windows she is opening one by one, each one offering only a fragmented view of the whole. Memories are the same, she thinks. They, too, come one by one and they too are connected. Through the labyrinth of her memory, through its many paths and crossroads, even though more than a decade separates them, Jerusalem meets California.

California – 1981 – RezaLeah

The street was no different from all the other streets of this sleepy Californian town where Marie had recently come in search of a new life: a tree-lined street with houses made of timber, all of them surrounded by exuberant and half-abandoned gardens, all of them a little worn out while exuding the quiet contentment of those who never think of moving somewhere else.

She checked the numbers on the doors: 2356, not far now. A few more yards, 2372, and then at last 2386. She hesitated. 'Her name is RezaLeah,' her friend Susan had said while jotting the phone number on a piece of paper. 'She is unusual,' Susan had warned, 'but I think she can help you.' Now could anyone really help her? Marie wondered. She felt so confused. America was too coarse, and Europe too demanding. She didn't quite know where she belonged. She shrugged then, filled with a mixture of dread and expectancy, knocked at the blue shabby door. A woman's voice urged her to come in.

Two months earlier, impulsively, Marie had left London behind, her friends, her family, her job. She wanted a larger life, she wanted freedom, and more than anything, she wanted to check that she could make it by herself. Life was too short for the series of comfortable habits, which until then was what she had made of her life: nice job in radio broadcasting, some good friends, a pleasant flat; but something was missing: love perhaps; a few short dissatisfying affairs were not enough. One should be able to wipe out the past and shape one's life anew, she believed. And what was there to preserve in her past? Not much. A recent holiday in San Francisco had convinced her that California was the place to start anew. She had a friend there who could shelter her for the first few days, and then she would start a business. Marie was good at making marmalade. The Americans liked English marmalade. So it was simple. She would make marmalade and sell it. Her friends in Paris had asked: 'Do you have enough capital to start a business? And a place? What kind of marketing will you do?' She found them annoying. Why so many questions? Of course she would manage. San Francisco was a beautiful and exciting city; what mattered in America was to be confident and she was, for her marmalade was really good. Her friends could testify to it.

Marie bought a large enough aluminium saucepan, and her new friends in the Berkeley hills, a doctor and his wife, gave her a whole load of 'decorative oranges' as the Americans call Seville oranges, the very ones bitter enough to make marmalade. All she needed was a lot of sugar and a lot of glass jars. What about labels, someone asked. Well, she will think about it later, and for the time being, before her business took shape, the three students she was tutoring in French gave her enough to survive. She now had her own flat, rented through the friend of a friend, and a kitchen large enough for her new venture.

Soon the flat was filled with the smell of oranges. Thankfully, she had not opted for fish soup or curry! But making marmalade is a lonely task. Marie had not thought of this. She sold a few jars to a bed & breakfast – they didn't mind the lack of labels as they emptied the marmalade into tiny little pots that had the advantage of looking good while limiting the amount of marmalade each customer was allowed. Most hotels, though, refused her marmalade as it had no guarantee from the health authorities; others complained that it was made with sugar, which was against all principles of healthy eating – well, she was in California!

Marie ended up selling her jars of marmalade at a flea market under a flyover near the San Francisco Bay, with the roar of traffic above her head, and on her rented stall, a sign announcing 'Genuine English Recipe'. People stopped, smiled at her then went on their way. A young bearded man shook his head in disapproval when Marie confessed that the making of marmalade required sugar. A woman in a bright red T-shirt, a baby tied on her chest, exclaimed, 'English marmalade! Is not American marmalade good enough?' Marie didn't argue. What was there to say? That actually the oranges were American? After four hours, tired from the heat and the dust, she'd sold a dozen jars. After two months, she came to the conclusion that making marmalade was too much of a lonely affair. She also had to admit she was no businesswoman. The aluminium saucepan went on a shelf and Marie knocked at the door of the Alliance Française. Teaching French was definitely easier and undoubtedly a more secure source of income than a marmalade business.

Years later, Marie was to smile at the naivety and blind faith of her younger self. Making marmalade on a large scale was not terribly enjoyable, after all. It took her some time to realize that what she was really good at was inventing stories, and that enacting them was usually not a very good idea, though it could lead to unexpected territories. For in the end, when everything went astray, a door did open and a brand new landscape appeared. As a child, she wanted to be an explorer, she wanted to get away, and in a sense, she had succeeded... several times. This last escape had not been very successful, though. Even she had to admit it. The sneaking feeling of unease she thought she had left behind had come back, and this time it couldn't be dismissed. More than ever she felt like a cork tossed helplessly in a river that seemed to carry her nowhere. It occurred to her that she needed direction. That's when Susan suggested she contact RezaLeah.

Paris 2014

Patricia laughs at her recounting. They are sitting in her kitchen, chatting over a cup of coffee. The sun is flooding the room and, as they often do, they are sharing their memories of years past. How foolish can one be, Patricia says, and tells her of the way she had met her husband. 'Such innocence! I knew nothing about men then,' and for a second, the smile of the young girl of half a century ago returns. But isn't it the way we all start, blindly innocent, stumbling through life and yet, miraculously, it seems, finding our way? Half to herself, half to Patricia, she asks, 'Could it be that our silly adventures, especially the ones that went wrong, were in fact shortcuts on the journey we don't even know we have undertaken?' Patricia looks at her, puzzled. 'What do you mean?' 'I mean that, for example, without this crazy attempt at starting a business – marmalade-making of all things – I wouldn't have sunk into a panic and met the person who would lead me to the very path I am still following to this day. She pauses and adds, 'Looking back, the cork – I mean myself floating on the current – may not have known where it was going, but somewhere its destination was already determined.' Patricia nods, unconvinced. 'You may be right,' she says with a sigh then, taking a sip of coffee, 'Do you think we ever learn?' she asks while carefully placing the cup back on its saucer. A bee buzzes through the open window then flies outside to the light. 'I don't know,' Marie says, 'probably not.' They look at each other and burst out laughing.

Paris 2014

What was it she was after in that month of May 1994? Her notes are difficult to read; the lines too close to each other, some words badly formed. Facts come to the surface but are drowned in the whirlpool of emotions that, at the time, hindered all her efforts at making sense of what was happening to her. As she reads, memories surge as vivid as if it had occurred the day before: her encounter with Ka-Tzetnik, the man who had survived Auschwitz, the discovery of the Convent of the Poor Clares, the meeting with Micheline, the brutal and sordid experience with the taxi driver, and of course the regular sessions with Gedaliah.

A pattern begins to appear: the energy field she had

accessed through RezaLeah then through Alex had spun threads that had reshaped her life. Those two people had opened the way to a journey that was nothing else than a search for the Absolute. Indeed, like a leitmotiv, a theme appears in the constant plea she made to all those she met in Jerusalem: please tell me that at the core of darkness, forever present, is a hidden light; please show me how to find that light in the darkness. The irony is that, caught as she was in her own drama, she was unaware that Gedaliah, the man she'd gone to for help, was offering her an answer. Not only was he repairing the damage, forcing her to re-examine Alex's spell, but he was showing her the Light on which to build a stronger identity. At the time, while drowning in a sea of pain, she was actually being reshaped. She had once prayed to be destroyed and made new – those had been her words – it had never occurred to her that being destroyed and being made new could be painful. And that it required time.

California – 1981

For several months, every week, Marie knocked at the blue shabby door behind which RezaLeah practised the subtle art of bringing people back to themselves. The woman was stooped, with the marks of age written on her face, yet her flaming hair and milky skin and that inner fire her eyes could not conceal suggested that she had once been a beauty. She kept her body hidden under long floating robes and some would have said that she looked like a witch. And in some way she was. Her whole person exuded a fierce energy, which probed through the knots and wounds that mould people's lives. Spending time with her was like exploring a familiar landscape, and then, to Marie's surprise, discovering new horizons in that landscape. Much of what Marie thought was hers she had borrowed from her mother: her leaning on appearances, her lack of confidence covered with false self-assurance, her need for approval. She began to emerge from the cocoon that, for years, had held her in crippling comfort. How do butterflies get their wings? How do they paint themselves in bright colours? No one really knows. Perhaps because no second birth ever takes place in full light, nor does it happen all of a sudden; rather it comes in slow bursts of consciousness, at times painful realizations, at times exhilarating insights, which together build a new, more real self.

One spring afternoon, RezaLeah asked, 'What would you do if you were told to jump off the Golden Gate Bridge?' Marie had walked across the famous bridge; she had looked down at the dark green, menacing sheet of metal. The thought of those poor people who threw themselves at it had made her shiver. Yet she didn't think twice. 'I would close my eyes and totally concentrate,' she said, 'and there would be no fear.' She caught the suggestion of a smile in RezaLeah's eyes. That day, she introduced Marie to a meditation technique: sitting back straight, legs uncrossed, feet on the ground, and, as much as possible, an empty mind. Until then, Marie had looked at people who meditated as half-witted, usually hippies. And there she was, sitting in her bedroom with, to her amazement, her mind filled with gratitude for giving it, at last, a break. Then she felt her whole body pulled upwards while her feet seemed to grow roots that nailed her to the floor. It was as if a powerful current was intent on stretching her. Even more astonishing, the experience felt like a homecoming.

Her relationship with RezaLeah took a different turn. The psychotherapist had become a spiritual guide, bringing a whole new flavour into Marie's life. On her promptings, Marie attended a piano master class, then met a group of writers and artists. During the Jewish holidays, she and RezaLeah attended a service at the reformed synagogue. Marie's world was expanding, it became more colourful, more alive; she had often sensed its richness but hadn't known how to enter it. One day RezaLeah took her to listen to a rabbi, 'an old friend of mine,' she said. His name was Gedaliah; he was originally from New York but now lived in Israel. A tall, large man, he carried that air of nonchalance that tells the world, 'I don't care how I look; I am well in myself.' He exuded serenity and goodness, a travelling craftsman offering his wares to whoever was willing to buy them. Not that his price was high; and not that what he was selling could be easily quantified, for his craft consisted in the telling of Hassidic tales, similar in many ways to the Sufi stories Marie had been reading and rereading for the last fifteen years. Like those stories, the tales talked of the fears and yearnings of human beings; like them, they resonated deep and sent ripples long after one had heard them, their wisdom inexhaustible. Marie went to several of Gedaliah's talks. There was some indefinable affinity between them even though their lives and backgrounds were far apart. On his way back to Israel, he usually stopped in London where he had friends and where, there too, his tales were gladly received. She took the address of the friend in England with whom he stayed. Just in case, she thought at the time.

And then there was that other afternoon, when sitting with RezaLeah, unexpected but undeniable, a sudden insight took Marie by surprise. She had got it wrong all along: God was not a judge as she had been made to believe. He was not the authority that delivered reward and punishment. The relationship with God was a love affair. Behind all our confusion and entanglements, He was the only object of our longing, of our desires, the true meaning at the core of all lives, calling us to return to Him. Overwhelmed, Marie closed her eyes while time expanded into no time. The silence in the room was alive, filled with invisible sparks. 'Go in peace,' said RezaLeah, when Marie stood up to leave.

Two winters went quickly, hardly winters under the Californian sky, except for the cold fog drifting over the Golden Gate Park. One February morning as the camellias exploded in various hues of red and pink, Marie had the inkling that it was time for her to leave and return to England. There were no real signs, just a hint that her Californian stay had fulfilled its purpose; that she had learnt all she could here. And, as if on cue, the gods intervened: a phone call from London with, at the other end of the line, a familiar voice asking, 'Marie, don't you think it's time for you to settle down?' And, without giving her time to reply, John, her ex-boss at the BBC World Service, added, 'I've just had a talk with personnel; there is an opening job in the Service and I thought of you.' The call didn't come as a complete surprise. Over the years, Marie had from time to time sent dispatches: about an international conference on Aids that had taken place in San Francisco, an interview with a jazz musician in Oakland, a short commentary on the multiculture of Californian universities. What surprised her was the feeling of relief that came over her. The prospect of a proper job was suddenly attractive again, and the words 'settle down', which, only a year ago, would have sent her into a panic, felt now reassuring. 'Yes, I think you're right,' she said. She had accepted and it felt right.

London – June 1983

As she passed through the door of Bush House, she had a moment of doubt. Was it a good idea to walk back into one's past? How many times would she go through that door again? Until retirement? The thought was unsettling. Nothing much had changed since the time – over nine years ago – when she had left for California. Outside the entrance, the plane trees still sent their shadows over the impressive stone building. At the reception, the porter hardly looked older and the two lifts still took their time to respond. She dismissed them and went straight to the staircase. Only two floors to go. But, as she climbed the stairs, she could tell she was not the same person. She was more confident, happier in herself. No, she was not entering the past even though a few of the old faces were still there, and apparently glad to see her. Others had retired or left for another job or, as expected, had died. But there were new ones, younger ones. Life had gone on here as well.

Once again she enjoyed her radio work: the research, the interviews, the mixing of words with music, even reading the news in the middle of the night when everyone else was in bed. England too was going through a new mood of optimism. Margaret Thatcher had just been re-elected. The Falklands War was over and won, the unions subjugated and, rightly or not, the country enjoyed a new sense of purpose. And then there was London, its theatres, its art galleries, the view of the City at dawn on Waterloo Bridge, the rhythms of the seasons, and, not to be despised, the security of a regular salary. The future looked bright. She now took time to meditate every day, RezaLeah's words still ringing in her ears, 'If you stop, you will soon start searching again.'

Looking at herself from a different perspective, Marie discovered, had unexpected repercussions. Doors that she didn't even know existed suddenly opened: a drawing class where art and wisdom subtly overlapped, an image coming to life under her pen once the ego had been temporarily put aside, people whom she would not have noticed only two or three years ago becoming close friends. One of them created strange sculptures out of rejects; another, to make ends meet, taught pottery in a secondary school, while at home he turned out magnificent pots, jugs and dishes, which he sold in the wealthy galleries of Mayfair or St John's Wood. Most of these people were involved in meditation; most of them struggled to make a living but they were alive and more real than most. The world had ceased to hurt; it had acquired a luminous quality and she was beginning to breathe more freely.

Every year, for a few weeks, Marie returned to California leaving behind the grey English skies and her busy London life. There she fell back into a world that knew little of clouds, where the hills smelt of lavender and eucalyptus. There she watched the ocean hammering the shore, enjoyed the sun and her friends and, of course, visited RezaLeah.

It was during one of these Californian escapes that she read a book in which the author recounted his meeting with a young Indian woman guru. The book carried an intense energy and from time to time, overwhelmed, Marie had to stop reading, as tears blurred her vision. One day, while alone with a friend, she felt herself overcome by a wave of tenderness of such power that she burst into tears. A tremendous feeling of love surrounded her and yet, incomprehensibly, seemed to surge within her. She tried to understand the experience. It's your imagination, she told herself, get back to earth. She could almost hear the words DON'T DOUBT. It was then that she decided that she would meet Alex, the author of the book.

London – 1991

On her return to London, she was told Alex was giving a talk the next day in a library in Camden. 'You should go and interview him,' a colleague suggested. Until then, Marie had always refused to mix her work with what she called her private life. The stirrings of the soul, she reckoned, were too intimate and too fragile to be exposed. Yet, this time, she thought, why not. She made contact with the author's agent and a meeting was agreed later in the week. In the meantime, she would go and listen to him in Camden.

A small crowd was already filling the lower level of the bookshop when she arrived, the upper level arranged as a stage for the speaker. He soon came up. Tall, dark eyes, his hair in the style of the sixties – longer than required by the fashion of the day – he was wearing a pair of jeans and a white turtleneck. Attractive, Marie thought. He started to talk and there were the same intensity, the same fierceness that filled his book. Marie was under his spell. Not everyone, though, was fascinated; some drifted away before the end of his talk. 'Too unbalanced, too much over the top,' one of them told her the following day.

Two days later, she was ringing the door of a flat near Sloane Square. A smiling Alex opened. 'Welcome, welcome,' he said leading her into a sitting room. She chose the sofa and he sat down in one of the two armchairs facing her. The room struck her by its lack of colour; everything was beige, cream or white, with an affectation of elegance devoid of life. A faint odour of disinfectant confirmed the impression that no one actually lived here. As if aware of her reaction, Alex explained that this was not his home. 'I am only staying here for a few days,' he said. She was somehow reassured. The place didn't fit with what she knew of him. It was just an empty shell while this man exuded a mixture of charm and self-confidence close to arrogance she found attractive. She didn't yet know this had more to do with a public school education than with his personality. But there was more to him than self-confidence and the desire to seduce. Sitting here with him, it was as if she had entered into a bubble of vibrant energy, an energy which made her more alive and filled her with an incomprehensible joy. It was intoxicating. He was looking at her, attentive yet relaxed. 'What shall we talk about?' he asked.

'Well, your book to start with.' Microphone in hand, the tape recorder resting beside her, she asked the obvious questions: how the book had come to be, how his encounter with this woman guru had affected his life. Soon the interview turned into a sharing of what appeared like a common thread running through their lives – a search for meaning and the Absolute. She closed the mic. He went and put a CD on the player. 'This will help,' he said without explaining how it would. They listened in silence to the violin, the notes rising higher and higher, stretching towards the infinite. She knew the piece: *The Protecting Veil* by John Tavener. A year earlier at the Albert Hall, she had heard it for the first time. 'This is the way,' she murmured. He nodded, 'Yes, and the journey has no end.' This curious feeling to know each other with hardly any need for words. He told her he lived in Paris in the Quartier Saint-Germain. Did she ever go to Paris? Actually, she was planning to be there two months later for a concert at the Chatelet theatre: *Cosi fan tutte* with John Eliot Gardiner conducting. 'Get two tickets,' he said promptly 'and we'll go together.' Still mesmerized, she left the flat, in a state of exhilaration. Their encounter was intended; it had been written in the heavens. She was almost dancing in the street. They would meet again; they would go to that concert together. And so it all began.

Years later, she still thought that it had been orchestrated from above: their meeting, their collaboration, as well as the end of the relationship. It had all gone so smoothly: their meeting in London then in Paris; the tickets for the concert – expensive ones – that came as free press tickets though she had never asked for them; Mozart's lightness and intensity that mirrored their own. After the concert, they walked along the Seine. The night was mild; it was spring. They talked of their search for God, he in India, she through the mystics of ancient Persia. He wanted to write a book on Sufism. He thought they might work together. The magic continued.

A month later, Alex organized the launch in London of a book on Tibetan teaching he had co-authored and Marie was among the guests. The crowd of people attending the launch were all involved one way or another in a spiritual quest. He phoned her the next day and mentioned the book he was thinking of writing. It was to be based on a series of lectures he had recently given in San Francisco on Rumi, the thirteenth century Persian mystic poet. Marie had known of these lectures; if she hadn't been tied by her work, she would have gone to San Francisco. Instead, she had suggested to her friend Joy, who lived across the Bay in Oakland, to go and listen to Alex. Joy did go to one of the talks, and dismissed it. 'Too excessive in tone,' she said afterwards. 'The man lacks sobriety.' Disappointed and upset, Marie shrugged away Joy's reaction. Joy simply didn't understand.

It took another eight months for the lectures to be transcribed. Then on a grey November day in 1993, the phone rang; it was Alex. He had the whole transcript in hand. Would she be ready to help and edit it with him? And if so, when would she be free to come to Paris? Marie still had some holiday in reserve. She could manage two full weeks in Paris, and probably arrange one more once back in London. 'Fine, wonderful!' Alex said. 'Let's start as soon as you can.' Ten days later, Marie was in Paris. A cousin of hers owned a studio near the Ecole Militaire. It was currently unoccupied and she could use it. Everything was in place.

Paris – December 1993

Alex was standing at the top of the narrow flight of stairs that prolonged the more spacious ones leading to the previous floors. He was wrapped in a black cape, a tall figure that could have been intimidating if not for his eyes smiling a welcome. She ignored the display and he quickly abandoned the cape. The flat consisted of a kitchen and a room that was almost filled with the bed and a desk squeezed in a corner near the window. In better times, the place would have been allocated to the servants who, during the day and often at night, worked on the lower floors. The building itself was one of those Hotels Particuliers that had long ago stopped being home to one family to be converted into separate flats. Inside the heavy gate that closed it to the outside world, there was a small door that Marie had pushed easily. A paved inner courtyard, in which a few meagre shrubs tried in vain to give the place a semblance of elegance, separated the building from the street. Two centuries earlier, this would have sheltered horses and carriages.

Alex lived on the top floor, the cheapest place an artist could afford in this part of Paris: Quartier Saint-Germain, on the left bank of the Seine. In the bedroom, pinned on the walls and set on every shelf were the faces of holy men and women, some smiling, some stern. A few of them Marie recognized: Sri Aurobindo,

Muktananda, Thomas Merton, the woman guru Ammaji known for hugging people and of course the woman who had prompted Alex to write the book she had read in California, the book that had led her to him. All of them silently proclaimed that here was a sanctuary and that, having had the privilege to enter it, she was now blessed.

They quickly got into a routine. Marie would arrive at nine. After a quick tea, Alex sat at his desk in the corner near the window, and she on the bed, propped up by two cushions, pencil in hand with the script of a lecture, each lecture corresponding to one chapter. Her task was to carefully edit each of them, and then pass it to Alex. The work was not dissimilar to the editing she was used to in her radio interviews. She saw at a glance the argument veering into unnecessary tangents, the repetitions concealed under the brilliance, the awkward sentence easy to correct. As the days succeeded each other, the room began to silently vibrate.

One morning, Marie brought a yellow rose that Alex placed in a vase on a table at the foot of the bed. After a day or two, the rose began to open and at the same time turned fiery. Then as it withered, its petals, instead of dropping, remained firmly attached, 'The heart is on fire,' Alex remarked.

During their short breaks, Alex would place a CD on the player and Janet Baker's voice filled the room with Handel's arias. They let the music enfold them then they resumed their work. 'Can I tell you something?' Marie would say from time to time as a thought crossed her mind. 'Yes...?' and as she spoke, Alex would reply, 'This is what I am just writing.' A sort of osmosis was taking place between them, the air in the room suffused by an invisible Presence. Marie had been searching for it in prayer, in dangerous confrontations, in sex, getting at times a sense of that Presence but unable to hold on to it. And here it was in the air they breathed, surrounding her, nourishing her, making her whole.

At noon, they went out for a quick meal to the small restaurant at the corner of the street where Alex as 'a regular' was attended like a king. The food was simple; peasant food made with good, earthy products. They ate voraciously, spoke nonsense, joked with the waitress. But they were hardly able to contain their impatience to re-enter the luminous Reality they had left behind.

For two weeks, day after day, they shared an intimacy of souls more intense than any sexual encounter could have ever been. Waking up one morning, Marie felt herself as if nailed to the bed, each cell of her body in ecstasy. It took her some time to be able to move and get ready. She arrived at Alex's flat still shaken by the experience. He greeted her with a glimmer of amusement in his eyes. He knew. She asked, 'Is this what you live with all the time?' He nodded half smiling. 'How do you manage?' 'You push it aside,' he said lightly and as though the experience was nothing special. He added, 'You get used to it.'

So went the days. At night, after a quick meal, they walked the streets, enjoying the crisp December air. They stopped at times in front of a shop window, here looking at a display of red and gold Venetian glasses shining in the semi-darkness, there at a group of reindeer jumping towards the sky in the window of the Bon Marché. They laughed like children at the Christmas glitter, the world outside a weak reflection of their inner world.

But as the days went by, a fear lurked. This wouldn't, couldn't last. Once the book was finished, Alex would go his way and Marie her own, and life would lose its shine. The thought terrified her. That evening, as she went to bed, two sentences, clear and precise, imprinted on her mind: *There will be more and more joy.* This was like a promise. And, *What you are seeking is within yourself.* She sat down on the bed, trembling. It was impossible to dismiss the message… but it seemed to tell her to let go of Alex, and that she couldn't. All she could do was to hold on to the moment. Forget about the future.

The two weeks were over; Marie had to leave. They had not quite finished. Alex would join her in London in a week so they could give the book its final touch. That last morning – she had come with her suitcase – they hugged each other then, together, walked down the stairs, crossed the inner courtyard, and then Alex hailed a taxi. The car, a dark blue sedan of an indefinite make, pulled up against the pavement. 'Can you take this lady to Roissy? Here is the fare.' The driver picked up her case and placed it in the boot; they hugged once again and she got into the taxi. As they drove off, Marie turned back but Alex had already disappeared into the building. She sank into her seat, already thinking of the week ahead when they would work together again in London.

The taxi had just left the Périphérique, the motorway that encircles the city and is supposed to ease the traffic in the centre of Paris. That morning, it was fluid, and as they left the belt rows of grey apartment blocks appeared on each side of the road. Both the driver and Marie were silent until he asked, 'Who was the man who paid for your fare?' Marie said he was a writer she had been working with on a book. The driver half turned to her, 'What's the book about?' Marie hesitated then, not sure how he would take it, 'It is about God,' she whispered. To her surprise, far from being ridiculed, her answer opened a floodgate. 'My girlfriend is dying,' the man blurted out, 'advanced leukaemia,' he added. Outside, the suburb had given way to the countryside; field after field of brown earth only interrupted from time to time by what looked like an abandoned house. 'We are both overwhelmed,' the man continued. 'I want to help her but I don't know how.' He spoke haltingly, close to tears. His emotion was contagious and she too felt close to tears. 'You must not despair,' she said. 'God is closer than you think.' They remained silent until, emerging from the morning mist, the airport appeared in the distance. She couldn't leave him like that. As they arrived, she asked the man to pull over and for a few minutes she tried to share with him some of the energy that had nourished her all those last two weeks. 'Give your girlfriend all your love,' she said. 'That's what she needs more than anything. This will help you too,' she added. He listened, like someone drowning or long deprived of food until they shook hands and she went her way.

As she entered the airport, she stopped, overcome by the harsh, feverish atmosphere. Her mind was still with the man in the taxi. This last encounter was no accident. Energy fields cannot but attract similar vibrations. Intensity calls for intensity. With Alex she had reached the only level of intensity worth having and she was still moving through its bubble. She walked towards the passport and customs officers, hardly aware of her surroundings. In less than two weeks, she and Alex would be working together again. For a second, she closed her eyes, submerged by a wave of gratitude. 'Your passport, Madame.' The immigration officer's voice sounded impatient. She wondered what he thought: another of those sleepwalking travellers, probably. She found herself in her seat with no memory of having boarded the plane. The man next to her was already plunged in his paper. Again she closed her eyes. This time nobody interfered.

London – December 1993

Alex had phoned the night before. It was her turn this time to greet him in her home. Her small flat near the Portobello Road was easily accessible from Kensington where he was staying. They adopted the same rhythm as in Paris: a full day's work, lunch, then at seven a walk through the surrounding streets. One afternoon, as they were reaching the end of their work, Alex disappeared and came back half an hour later carrying a teapot, two candlesticks and a large Indian cup and saucer, all of them in engraved coloured metal. 'This is for you,' he said. She laughed. Couldn't he do anything without overdoing it? And then, there had been that time, in the late afternoon – they were both tired –

when they argued about some innocuous question and ended up wrestling and giggling on the carpet. Then all of a sudden Alex froze and together they stood up. None of them spoke but they knew. Entangled as it is with the soul, the body doesn't like to be ignored. 'I wish you were old and ugly,' Marie had once said to Alex who was stretching nonchalantly on the sofa in the Kensington flat where they had met to discuss their collaboration. 'Oh,' Alex had laughed, 'that will come soon enough.' She too had laughed. There was no harm in letting him know that she found him attractive; it was tacitly agreed that their relationship, however professional, was also one of friendship and that, for the sake of their work together, they wouldn't cross the threshold.

On their last evening, as they walked round the block, Alex said he would like their collaboration to continue; he had other projects in mind. One of them was a book of quotations of Rumi. That would mean a lot of research. What did she think? It was exactly what Marie had been wishing for: a close working association with Alex. Of course, she would work with him. Why even ask? 'Good,' Alex said, 'and in the meantime I have two tickets for tomorrow night at the Queen Elizabeth Hall: Monteverdi's *Coronation of Poppea*, John Eliot Gardiner conducting.'

A chatty and noisy crowd was already filling the lobby when they arrived, and soon the bell sounded, urging people to go and take their seat. It was one of those special evenings; Bob Geldof was supposed to be among the audience. Not that it mattered. What mattered was that Alex was sitting beside her and that the music that filled the hall was sublime. This couldn't be said of the story: Nero getting rid of his wife and stealing his officer's wife Poppea; rather shabby really. Marie chose to ignore the plot; the music was carrying only one message, love. And wasn't love everything? The final duet between Nero and Poppea was pure love-making. The two voices caressed each other, mingled then separated only to return to a new embrace. Marie was close to fainting. The voices expressed everything she and Alex had shared these last three weeks, their intimacy at a level far beyond the physical, a melting of the souls that only music could express. She was still trembling when they came out of the concert hall. Around them, hurrying away, people were talking, laughing. Marie couldn't say a word. It was high tide and a few feet away a shimmering Thames was lapping the shore, the London night and its reflection sparkled with lights. Hand in hand, they crossed the Charing Cross Bridge. Once on the Strand, Alex put her in a taxi. It was almost a relief to be alone again. Being with him was like being wired to the grid; it was exhausting, his energy hard to contain. She needed intervals of solitude; she needed to breathe more lightly out of his presence. The thought felt vaguely disloyal.

Paris 2014

She can't help noticing after all those years that her view of Monteverdi's opera somehow reflected her frame of mind at the time. How easily it was to confuse passion with love, and intense emotions with spiritual experience. That day at the Queen Elizabeth Hall, she deliberately chose to concentrate on Monteverdi's music and to discard the crude reality of Nero and Poppea's love affair. In his Masnavi, Rumi quotes God saying, 'You are in love with your state; you are not in love with Me.' She knew the quote but it didn't seem to apply to what she had felt for Alex.

December 1993

It was time to say goodbye. In two days, Alex was leaving for San Francisco where he would meet his publisher and organize another series of talks. They met one more time in Kensington and together went to the EMI music shop on the High Street. Alex wanted to buy her a piece of early music sung by the Tallis

Scholars, a Mass by the fifteenth century composer Josquin des Prés. He found it. As they left the shop, he stopped on the edge of the pavement and handed her the CD. She expected him to give her a last goodbye hug, but instead, as they faced each other, he placed his hand on her heart and left it there for what seemed a long time. 'I'm not sure I should let you do that,' Marie said, but didn't push his hand away. For the next three days, she hardly ate and slept. It was like having a fever without being ill. She had no doubt; this was Alex's work, that he had transmitted to her heart some of the powerful energy he was carrying. As she asked herself how one lives with such energy, she could hear Alex's voice again, 'You just push it aside, that's all.' At work, people remarked on her radiating happiness. She certainly had never been filled with such exhilarating joy before. At night, she thought of her next meeting with Alex in less than three months in California, of the many books they would write together. Their association was only beginning. She might have to leave her job... a whole new life was waiting.

California – February 1994

The flight to San Francisco went smoothly. But the half hour before landing seemed to last forever. This visit to California would be very different from the previous ones. This time, Alex was there. She couldn't wait to see him again. He had found a small flat in the centre of San Francisco. She, for her part, would stay with a friend on the other side of the Bay, but of course, they would see each other every day.

Alex was busy meeting people and organizing a new series of lectures; he didn't know how to drive and needed someone to drive him around. Would she? he asked. She didn't mind; on the contrary. This was another opportunity for being with him. He introduced her to his publisher. 'Without Marie,' he said, 'this book wouldn't exist.' Yes, she thought, it had been such a team work. But things had changed. There was now a distance between them. He was nervous, impatient. Once, on returning from Sausalito, she took the wrong exit to San Francisco and he complained bitterly that he was going to be late. Their old complicity seemed to have vanished. Another time, she'd made fun of his love of exaggeration. 'My suffering is bigger than yours,' she said laughing, mimicking him. He didn't laugh but remained sullen. Was he sulking? She wondered. In Paris and London, God had been the link between them; but here it was less clear. God had receded; only Alex mattered. When with friends, Marie was unable to talk about anything but him. Appalled and bored, friends listened in silence. Wasn't there more to life than Alex? one of them dared ask. But Marie was unreachable. RezaLeah, for her part, seemed impressed by her connection with a writer of some fame. Or was she trying to channel Marie's attention in a different direction? She mentioned an author she knew in Israel, a man who had been in Auschwitz and had survived the camp. 'You could go and interview him,' she suggested. 'He used to be called Yehiel De-Nur,' she said, 'but that was before Auschwitz.' All that was left of the man's identity was the German word for the inmate of a concentration camp, Ka-Tzetnik, followed by the number tattooed on his left arm. All his books – all of them dealing with the camps – were signed thus. 'He lives in Tel Aviv,' RezaLeah said. She gave Marie his address and lent her his books. They described in minute detail the nightmare millions of people had gone through. This was not particularly new to Marie. She had already read numerous books about the Holocaust, seen the films and the photographs: the emaciated bodies, the shaved heads and the eyes empty of life. She worried at times: Why this fascination? Was it a kind of morbid indulgence? But no, the horror and the shame must not be forgotten, they must be told for the generations to come. RezaLeah's suggestion didn't seem a bad idea, even though the thought of meeting a man who had survived the horror, and then to write about him, filled her with fear. But infused with Alex's energy, Marie could contend with any fear or doubt. When she mentioned the idea, Alex approved, adding, 'While you're there find yourself a sexy rabbi.' The remark was as incongruous as it was insulting. Was it a way of acknowledging the sexual tension between them, which they had carefully kept at bay? She ignored the remark. She now had a project he found worthwhile. That was all that mattered. Dismissing the unease of the recent weeks, she let the remark pass.

Her stay in California was approaching its end. It was time, Alex said, to sign a contract for the book of Rumi's quotations, which they would co-author. They went together to his publisher where she put her signature beside Alex's. Back in England, Marie would begin to do the research. This was more than a contract; this sealed their collaboration for the years to come.

The next day, Alex announced they were to have dinner at a well-known restaurant with his publisher and his editor. She was first to meet Alex at his flat. When she arrived, he had just opened a bottle of champagne. They finished the bottle. It didn't seem to affect him but Marie's head was spinning, and all evening, she struggled to stay alert. She ate and stayed mostly silent, nodding at times, pretending to understand what was being said. She would have liked to have taken part in the conversation but really, she wasn't interested; it all felt so irrelevant. Like a child, she listened to the grown-ups talking about things she didn't much care for: publishing trends, the marketing of books, what made a best-seller. When from time to time Alex asked for her opinion, her thoughts came tumbling in disarray only to drift away as soon as she tried to articulate something sensible and she ended up mumbling a banality.

As they left the restaurant, Alex felt obliged to mention her project in Israel, as if to say, Look, she is not as inept as she appears. On the way, while she drove him back home, he reproached her. 'You could have participated some more to the conversation. You hardly spoke.' She felt guilty and insufficient;

she had failed him.

They parted a few days later. Their next encounter, four months later, would be when working together again on Rumi's quotations.

In London, Marie went back to her radio work while preparing for her trip to Israel. At times she had doubts. What would she write? What would she ask Ka-Tzetnik? Was she really up to the task? But the thought of Alex brought back her confidence. He had approved of her project. Everything would be all right. In an exchange of letters, Ka-Tzetnik said he was willing to meet her but made it clear it wouldn't be for an interview about him. He was prepared, though, to help her write a book on the Holocaust. She would think about it in Israel. She bought her ticket. She'd be there in two months.

London – April 1994

It must have been around five o'clock in the afternoon. The sun was still high above the roofs. Marie loved the spring in London, the blue clusters of wisteria clinging to the houses and the sudden whiff of lilac that caught you by surprise at the corner of a street. She pushed up the sash of the kitchen window and tested the earth around the rose on the windowsill with her finger. Dry of course. It hadn't been raining for days. The rose, she noticed, already had three buds. She picked up an earthen jug from the shelf and filled it with water. She was beginning to pour the water when the phone rang. It might be Alex. It was a woman's voice. 'Oh, Cynthia, what a surprise! How are you?' Cynthia, an acquaintance, lived in California. Why would she contact her? 'It's about Alex,' Cynthia said without any preliminary. There was no trace of the happy, chatty woman Marie remembered; the voice was serious, almost solemn. 'I thought you should know,' said Cynthia. Marie's heart sank. 'What about Alex? Is he well?' 'I suppose so,' said Cynthia, 'but he is going around saying he doesn't want to have anything to do with you, that you've betrayed him. I thought you should know,' she repeated. Marie choked on her tears. 'I don't understand. What does he believe? What have I done?' 'I don't know,' said Cynthia. 'I just wanted you to know,' then, 'I'm sorry. Bye, Marie.' The click at the other end of the line, then the void. There was nowhere to flee, nowhere to stop the blade from stabbing her.

She phoned San Francisco. California was eight hours behind England; he might be there. The phone rang, once, twice, three times, then Alex's voice on the answering machine. Half in tears, she let the words pour out. 'Alex, please answer me. We are one; we can't be separated. You know that.' That night, she hardly slept. It crossed her mind to call work and say she wasn't feeling well. Hardly a lie. Yet having people around would to some extent help keep in check the storm raging in her mind. But once in front of her desk, she was unable to think of anything but Alex. She wrote him a message: 'Alex, what is it you think I have done? I love you, you know it. Don't you remember Paris and our work together?'... She stopped herself. The message had to be short if he were to read it, more like an SOS. She phoned Federal Express, the same courier she had seen him use to contact his publisher in the States. The courier would be at the main entrance in less than ten minutes. She ran through the corridors with her letter, rushed down the stairs to the main reception desk. The young man, his helmet under his arm, took the letter and handed her a document to sign. There it was, in a few hours, Alex would have her letter.

The days were devoid of colour, devoid of flavour. She did several interviews about the government policy towards the unions, about the current relations between the West and 'the man one can do business with' as Margaret Thatcher called Gorbachev, the new Soviet leader. She wrote weekly press reviews, did a programme on Aids in Africa. It kept her mind occupied for a while but did nothing to alleviate the haunting absence of Alex, his silence – for he hadn't replied. Several times a day, she would stop and look into a mirror, at work, at home, in the panes of a shop window, checking she still existed. Every time she was taken by surprise: the person looking back at her was the same middle-aged woman, tall and slim with chestnut hair and a tired face. Was this her? Was this how she looked? Dreams filled her nights, messages to hold on to in the stormy sea of her grief. In one of these dreams, she was trying to leave a train station, but outside, clouds of scorching steam barred the road, a murderous breath gushing every two seconds from the nuclear power station nearby. To try to pass? She would be swept away by the fiery steam. She had no other choice but to remain where she was. In another dream, the train she'd been on had left and now, abandoned on the other side of the track on a heap of muck, she was waiting for the train coming from the opposite direction. Left on the dirt was a small golden key, waiting for her. Powerful dreams, meaningful dreams, whose messages were almost lost on her in the storm that raged within. Only one thing mattered: to see Alex again, to re-establish the connection. It crossed her mind that an addict deprived of drugs must feel the same. Alex was her addiction; to live without him was unbearable. Marie thought of catching a flight to the States. She knew he was soon to give a talk at the Smithsonian Institute in Washington. She had friends there she could stay with. Yet, was it the warning in the dreams? She didn't buy a ticket.

She vaguely remembered that in the Sufi tradition, the word 'station' means the psychological place where the disciple must remain until the necessary knowledge has taken root; that, under the protection of the Masters, the 'station' is where the teaching takes place.

Several weeks later a letter arrived, not from Alex but from his San Francisco publisher. With shaking hands, she tore open the envelope. The letter was short. Alex wouldn't work with her again and asked not to be contacted. His decision, the letter said, was 'irrevocable'. The word branded itself on her mind. As for the contract, it was now null and void. Impossible to go on pretending that nothing had happened, that one day Alex would change his mind. She let the letter drop from her hands.

Tel Aviv – May 1994

'You are not eating?' said the man sitting next to Marie. He was about forty, greyish hair and not on the thin side, apparently concerned at her lack of appetite. 'No, I'm not hungry. Would you like some?'

'Oh, no! I didn't mean that,' he said his face turning red.

'It's all right. I won't eat any of it. I'm not hungry,' she repeated. She couldn't tell him that since Cynthia's phone call, she had hardly slept or eaten, that the very thought of food made her stomach churn. 'It's better not to waste all of it,' she added to ease his embarrassment. He gave her a smile and picked the small pot of cream with the biscuit. 'Thank you.'

She nodded and turned towards the window. Small white fluffs of cloud were floating over the wings of the plane, which drifted away in the blue of the sky. She didn't really want to go to Israel. She didn't really want to go anywhere. It all felt so meaningless. But she had bought the ticket and Ka-Tzetnik had agreed to meet her. She was to call him on arrival. She sighed. Well, it was all going to happen, after all. They would meet five or six times; she would take notes and, out of her notes, a book would emerge. She let herself dream. Once published, she would send the book to Alex; he would be impressed; he would contact her and say it was all a mistake… She closed her eyes, her heart soothed by the dream and the purr of the engines. A few minutes later, a tap on her arm startled her. 'Excuse me, this lady wants your tray,' her companion indicated the air hostess standing by his seat. Marie handed over the untouched tray and closed her eyes again. A voice announced they would be at Ben Gurion Airport in half an hour. 'The temperature in Tel Aviv is thirty-two degrees,' the voice added.

Israel was in the grip of a heatwave, and in Tel Aviv, air saturated with humidity made the heat fierce. To make things worse, the cheap hotel Marie had found in the centre had no air conditioning and the size of the only room available allowed hardly any space between the bed and the narrow wardrobe. The view from the window was blocked by a concrete wall that let in just enough light for someone not to bump into the furniture, and the bathroom was accessible from the corridor. But the thought of going in search of another hotel was too much. The only thing she wanted was sleep.

She woke up in a sweat. The air had barely cooled down during the night. She pulled a white summer dress out of her suitcase, and after a quick shower got out to face the day. She didn't feel ready to call De-Nur. Tomorrow, she thought. In the meantime, she would try to orientate herself; perhaps take a walk on the seafront.

She stopped at a French café where she ordered a freshly squeezed orange juice and a croissant. The silent couple at the table next to her – the woman, dyed blond hair, friendly eyes, her husband, white hair neatly parted – didn't quite look like tourists. They must have been in their sixties. 'Is the sea very far?' asked Marie.

'No, not far at all,' said the woman, who welcomed the opportunity to chat. The husband nodded in assent. The woman's name was Marie-Louise. She was born in Germany but she had been one of the lucky ones. 'My father decided to go to Palestine in 1936,' she said, then, after a pause, added with a sigh, 'just in time'. The rest of her family had disappeared in the camps. 'And this is Geoffrey,' said Marie-Louise, as if suddenly remembering her husband. 'We met here in Tel Aviv,' she said as she brushed an invisible speck of dust on her husband's blazer. A smile lit her face at the memory. 'We now live in Toronto,' she continued, 'but we come here every year for two or three weeks, our little honey-moons,' she added with a girly chuckle.

How many stories were concealed behind the faces of all those people passing by? Marie wondered. As though answering her thought, 'You know, Léon, the owner of this café,' Marie-Louise was saying, 'he used to live in France but he received so many threats there that in the end, he decided to move to Israel.' Marie sighed.

'I didn't realize there was still so much anti-Semitism in France. I am French, you see.' Thankfully, Marie-Louise was not interested in what had brought her to Tel Aviv. Marie made a move. 'You said the sea was not far?'

'No, not far at all,' repeated the woman. 'You'll be there in five minutes. Follow this avenue then take the first right; the sea will be a few hundred yards.'

On the seafront, however, all there was to see was a row of giant hotels: Sheraton, Holiday Inn, Ramada, with, between the concrete blocks, narrow glimpses of blue. As she approached one of the giants, the red-liveried porter bowed and opened the door. She took a few steps in and for a moment stood looking at the wide armchairs, the large sofas carefully arranged around equally large coffee tables. Wide panes of glass overlooked a beach spread with white mattresses and orange parasols under which lay a few tanned bodies. At last, she could gaze at the open sea, but the soulless atmosphere of the place made her flee. She walked along the buildings and came to a larger gap of shimmering blue – a small Mediterranean garden, with an olive tree and a stretch of fragrant herbs overlooking the vastness of the sea. On the twisted trunk, an engraved copper plaque gave the name of the Muslim saint buried on this spot. Marie sent a silent prayer to the saint. She had been told that in Israel, building on consecrated land was not permitted; but apparently barring the view to the sea was allowed! She spent the rest of the morning roaming the streets. But wherever she went, Alex's absence weighted on her until, exhausted by the heat, she stopped at a small restaurant for a bowl of soup, and then retreated to her hotel.

Ka-Tzetnik

The three-storey building of creamy stones stood in a quiet area in the centre of Tel Aviv shadowed by the blue-purple haze of jacarandas trees, with here and there a tired, dusty hibiscus shrub dotted with dark, red weathered flowers. 'Two-thirty this afternoon,' he'd said that morning on the phone. 'You have my address; I am on the second floor.' The voice was matter of fact, giving no hint of mood or feeling.

The rusty wrought iron door opened with a groan. Inside, the white tiled panelled walls were more reminiscent of a swimming pool or bathroom than of a block of flats. No trace of a lift. She walked up the stairs, her mind empty. There was only one door on the landing, with the expected mezuzah on the right side of the frame. She pressed the bell and the door opened.

He was smaller than she had expected. Dressed in white, the sleeves of his shirt rolled over, a black skullcap too small to hide his baldness, he gestured her to enter. His green-blue eyes were unsmiling yet welcoming. There was no entrance hall; they were standing in a kitchen, with a rectangular pine table, four chairs, and, fixed on the walls, three cabinets of indeterminate colour. 'Please do sit down,' he said, himself taking the chair facing her. She looked round, no sign of food or dishes anywhere. 'I have read your books,' she started. He nodded, waiting for her to continue. She felt embarrassed, her mind suddenly blank. What was it she wanted from him? One thing she knew: there was no place here for pretence or half-truth. She began again. 'I don't really know what it is I want from you,' she confessed. She stopped, not sure this was the best way to start. Then the words burst out of her. His book, *Shivitti*, sprang to her mind. Of all the books she had read on the Holocaust, *Shivitti* had been the only one which had left a lasting impression. 'What I know, what I believe,' she said, 'is that, hidden at the core of darkness, there is something sacred, a light. That light shines bright in *Shivitti*.' The man remained silent. Only his eyes indicated that he was listening.

The book had surged out of the treatment with LSD he had undertaken several years earlier in the Netherlands with a Dutch psychiatrist. It was strange to think that here, sitting in front of her, was the same man who had gone through that treatment and written *Shivitti*. She looked at his hands resting on the table, fine and sensitive, almost translucent. Words now came easily. 'In this book, you talk of the spark you still carry with you "when you are shorn of all", you talk of the "spark leaping from the smokestack." But,' she was begging him, 'how do we reach this spark in the depth of darkness? How can we be the spark?' He didn't seem shocked or surprised at her question. Once again he nodded. 'I understand,' he said. Then, 'Every day I write, and the next morning I burn it all,' his voice low, yet clear. He smoothed an invisible line on his brow and shook his head. 'But it is not this, it is not that.' The silence in the room was palpable; she felt it weaving invisible threads that seemed to be building a fragile bridge between them. She could feel his despair, as intense as his determination. She knew he wouldn't stop writing. 'I see their eyes,' he went on, 'I see the look in their eyes as they walk to the gas chamber, to the inferno.' She too nodded. She understood. He was trying to give a human voice to what no one could comprehend and no word could contain. The task was barely human, probably impossible. It occurred to her that they were on a similar quest, the search for the light he had glimpsed in the depth of darkness, the Presence she sensed within herself at the core of her pain but didn't know how to reach.

Wasn't that the paradox that mystics of every tradition try to convey when they assert that annihilation and fulfilment are one? Many years earlier she had visited Dachau, the camp the

Nazis had opened in 1933, and where a prayer had sprung to her lips, 'Please forgive us.' Us, not them, for they were all guilty, the whole of humanity was guilty. She had wanted to kneel there on the spot, too self-conscious to do so but glad, a few minutes later, to find the small chapel where she had fallen on her knees. And then, around the same time, on her television screen, the woman in brown rags standing amidst a brown landscape, a dead child in her arms – Ethiopia 1984 – there again, the same impulse to kneel, the same feeling of sacredness. The image had stayed with her.

Calm and apparently unmoved, he was looking at her. 'I'm sorry,' he said, shaking his head. 'I can't help you.' And after a pause, 'We won't meet again. I have my work to continue.' She was surprised at how easily she accepted his refusal, perhaps because it was not so much a refusal as an acknowledgment of inability. She'd thought she would be afraid of him but, far from fear, what she felt for this man was deep love and a huge respect. She felt like crying.

They both stood up at the same time and he took her to the door. She was still feeling the touch of his hand when the door closed behind her. She walked down the stairs in a daze. Outside, the heat felt like a cloak of lead. Nothing had changed. Why should it? The streets and the jacarandas were still there, the buildings around just as banal as before, and the hibiscus flowers still looked like bloodstains on the dusty shrubs. The ordinariness of the scene was as much a relief as an assault. A few people passed by, taking no notice of the woman standing there, none of them aware that a few yards away, on the second floor of one of these ordinary buildings, a man was silently screaming. She felt drained. What to do? There was nowhere to go, nobody to call upon. Jerusalem, the name jumped at her. She had been there three years earlier with RezaLeah. She remembered the city, its centuries-old streets, its walls as ancient as humanity. She knew a few people there; among them, Gedaliah, the rabbi whom she had first met in California then later in England. There was no point staying in Tel Aviv. She returned to her hotel, paid her bill, and went in search of a coach that would take her to the ancient city.

Jerusalem – May 1994

It was just before dusk when the coach entered Jerusalem. Outlined on the sky, the ramparts of the Old City stretched in a blaze of golden light. Jerusalem! After the blank anonymity of Tel Aviv, it was a balm on the heart. She wouldn't look for a hotel, she decided. A convent would suit her better; it would also be cheaper. She hailed a taxi. Yes, he knew of a convent. 'It's right in the centre,' said the driver, 'the Convent of the Sacred Heart.' Would that be OK? He dropped her with her suitcase in front of a wooden gate that showed no visible way of getting open. The taxi was still there; helpless, she looked at it. 'You must ring the bell,' the driver said pointing at the right side of the gate. Marie nodded a thank you. She must really be tired, she thought; the hand bell, a dark knob on the white wall, was quite discernible. She pressed it and, after a few minutes, an unsmiling woman garbed in black unlocked the gate. The taxi had disappeared. Yes, there were rooms available. The nun let Marie in and carefully relocked the door behind them. They were in a barren courtyard that led to an austere stone building, darkened by the ages. Inside, near the entrance, a table and a chair served as reception desk. 'The room is thirty-five dollars a night,' said the nun dryly after she'd taken Marie's details. She then indicated a large staircase. 'I'll show you your room,' she said, 'come with me.' She began walking up the stairs followed by Marie. On the first floor, they entered a corridor lined on both sides by doors. Marie counted six of them. The room was the last on the left. 'Here is your key,' the nun said, as Marie entered the room. Inside was a bed, a wooden desk, a chair and a cheap wardrobe made of plywood. 'The front gate closes at ten every evening.'

The nun looked at Marie as if she suspected her of planning to spend her nights in sin. 'No one is allowed in or out after that time.' She gave Marie a last suspicious look then shuffled away. Not the warm welcome one expects from a convent. Marie dropped her suitcase on the floor and peered through the window; all she could see was the empty courtyard over which a crescent moon threw a ghostly light. The place felt more like a prison than a convent, and the curfew was rather inconvenient. She must look for somewhere else; there should be other convents that were more welcoming. And next morning, she would also phone Gedaliah. A feeling of warmth came over her at the thought of his face.

At least the bed was not uncomfortable and Marie managed to get a few hours' sleep. Considering the heat, the fact that the shower offered only cold water was not too inconvenient. Breakfast for the paying guests, of whom she seemed to be the only one, was not part of the deal. Fortunately, there was a café nearby. After a glass of orange juice followed by a coffee, she walked down a slope through a cluster of small houses and gardens. High above her the Old City spread its ramparts. She entered the Jaffa Gate and stopped. It was all so familiar. Here was the same Middle East she had found in Turkey, in Syria, in Jordan; the same smell of charcoal, of spices, of rotten fruit, and the call to prayer, but here mingling with the bells of hundreds of churches and monasteries. She took in the scene: the souvenir shop and their posters advertising the rates of exchange, the post office for the tourists to send their postcards, the lanes sinking into dimness. The one in front of her wound its way through stalls of fruit sellers and small shops that looked more like caves. The shops were filled with the paraphernalia of tourist knick-knacks but they also hid, she had been told, real antiques. Under her feet, the slabs of stones wore the marks of wheels that had run there for millennia. She asked her way a few times and noticed that the maze of narrow lanes had imperceptibly changed from Christian to Muslim then Jewish. Men, the fringes of their prayer shawls hanging from under black coats, were now passing her, all seemingly in haste to reach their destination. Gedaliah of course lived in the Jewish quarter. 'Come to my home at eleven,' he'd said on the phone, and here she was, her heart so heavy that she had to stop to recover her breath; still, the thought of Gedaliah's friendly face offered a faint light in the dark tunnel of her grief and loneliness.

She had no idea what to expect when she rang the bell. He took her to the same small room where he had received her two days earlier. They sat facing each other and once again, she poured her pain out, the unbearable loss of Alex. Gedaliah let her talk, then 'Close your eyes,' he said. 'Now tell me, how big is the pain? Which colour?' It was not difficult to see it; it was hard, heavy, a black, sharp-pointed stone; it had dropped from the sky and dug into her flesh. 'Remove the flesh and pull the stone out,' said Gedaliah. 'Do it slowly, carefully, not to hurt.' Marie could see her fingers gently pushing the flesh out of the way then extracting the stone. The feeling of heaviness began to dissipate but the flesh was left raw. Under Gedaliah's guidance, she sprinkled the wound with a white powder. 'Now to heal the wound, bring the Light on it. See each cell coming back to life under the Light; see the cells growing again, see the wound filled with new healthy flesh.'

Modern psychologists, Marie later found, acknowledge what the mystics in all traditions have always known, that what the mind visualizes, it understands as real. She also discovered that healing through Light is part of the Kabbalah, the ancient Jewish mystical tradition.

During her stay in Jerusalem she went to see Gedaliah several times a week. With him as her guide, she washed in the sea, climbed mountain peaks, retraced her steps through the alleyways of her childhood. She saw the blind alleys her mother had led her to, looked at her father's loneliness. Exposed was the guilt she had been carrying for so long, her contempt for her father, her blind imitation of her mother. Astonished, she discovered that, all along, love had always been there, a love that none of them quite knew how to give or receive. She lay on the grass of meadows flooded by sun, she washed herself in rivers of pure crystalline water, dressed herself in new radiant clothes; she called to God.

Jerusalem – May 1994

She left the coffee shop, walked for a while down a large avenue and finally hailed a taxi. Could he take her around and show her Jerusalem? 'I only know the Old City,' she said. The driver, a young man with dark, wavy hair and hazel eyes, seemed proud to show his city and was obviously glad to have a client that would earn him more than the usual short errand. They passed old houses half hidden in lush gardens with next to them rising buildings of white stones, ready to smother the old Jerusalem in soulless modernity. He took her to the Hebrew University on Mount Scopus and to the Israel Museum where, next to the main building, stood wide open as if hastily abandoned an enormous white umbrella. 'This,' the driver said, 'is the Shrine of the Book.' This was where the Dead Sea Scrolls were kept, he told Marie. She was vaguely interested, but not enough to go inside and have a look. They stopped in front of the great synagogue but she didn't think it was appropriate for her to go in. At some point, they slowed down along a crowded market, the stalls loaded with an abundance of fruit and vegetables. They exchanged a few banalities, each of them locked in a world foreign to the other. But she was a woman and he was a man, and at some point, after he'd stopped the car and as they stood over a stone balustrade looking over the city down the valley, he made a move towards her and she let him touch her breast. If that is what he wants, Marie thought, why not? Again, the feeling that nothing mattered, that somehow she didn't even exist. He drove her back to the convent. Aware of the implication, she agreed to meet him again the following night. He would be waiting for her in front of this same gate, he said. She looked at the car driving away. Not exactly the 'sexy rabbi' Alex had recommended.

It was still early and she went in search of a kebab restaurant for a meal before the convent curfew. There was nothing special about the one she found in a street nearby: just a narrow space filled with two small tables and four chairs. On the menu were the usual Middle Eastern salads, fried aubergines, lamb and falafel. She chose a mix of them stuffed into pita bread which she ate rapidly before walking back to the convent. The idea of spending another night in this prison was hardly bearable. Tomorrow, she would look for another place.

The Convent of the Poor Clares

The Convent of the Poor Clares was located on a hill, not far from the centre. The woman at the tourist office had said that the nuns were French and that they welcomed paying guests. Marie was soon ringing the bell of another locked gate.

The contrast couldn't have been greater after the stern rigidity of her previous lodgings. Here was an oasis of peace and gentle beauty, the nuns as welcoming as she had been told. The tall and friendly woman who let Marie in said that, yes, there was a room available, and then took her through the overgrown garden that surrounded the convent until they reached a small building. They stopped in front of four steps leading to a door half barred by honeysuckle that seemed to have planted itself here just to make sure it would get attention. 'This is the room,' said the nun as she opened the door. 'By the way, my name is Sister Blandine. The room is very simple but I hope it will suit you.' Marie smiled back. 'This is perfect,' she said, looking at the whitewashed walls, the white coverlet on the bed with the crucifix above it. 'The bathroom is right there,' said Sister Blandine, as she opened a second door inside the room. 'How many days will you stay?' I could stay there forever, Marie thought. 'About two weeks, a bit more, I think.' She had not counted the days.

Later on, without mentioning any curfew Sister Blandine gave Marie a key to the front gate. 'Be careful to lock the door when you go out and after you come in,' she said. Marie took the key and went in search of a meal. She was glad to return to the unadorned simplicity and peace of her bedroom. But even here, there was no escape. In the stillness of the night, more acute than ever, the stabbing pain was still there. And now she had this appointment with the taxi driver. It didn't really make sense but it was still early and she had nothing else to do. She went out again and walked down the hill towards her previous lodgings. The taxi was already there when she arrived. He didn't move from behind the wheel but leant over to open the door. They exchanged greetings and he immediately started the engine. She vaguely wondered where he was to take her but didn't care and didn't ask. A numbness, a fatalistic disinterest as to what could happen to her had taken over. They quickly left the inhabited areas and took a road that went uphill. Neither of them spoke.

The Convent of the Poor Clares

Apart from Marie, there were two other guests at the convent, both French. There was Olivier, who had walked all the way from Europe to Jerusalem and made of his life a continuous prayer. A simple man, he made no demand, carried no judgement and didn't show any hint of self-consciousness or pretence. Probably in his late thirties, his solid presence made you quickly forget the details of his appearance: short reddish hair, square jaw and a stocky body. Only the shine in his eyes was arresting. Marie talked to him a few times but they were too far apart – he seemed to have found his way – she was stumbling in the dark.

The other guest was Micheline, a woman born seriously

handicapped, whose life was a constant struggle against isolation and rejection. Sister Blandine had mentioned her, saying that Micheline always enjoyed meeting new people, a faint hint at suggesting that a visit by Marie would soothe some of the woman's loneliness.

Though warned by Sister Blandine, it was still a shock when she saw the frail and thin woman in her wheelchair whose contorted smile didn't quite soften the grunt with which she welcomed Marie. Her body reminded her of the olive tree with its distorted trunk on the seashore in Tel Aviv. Micheline could have been forty or perhaps fifty; it was difficult to tell. The face, hardly creased, gave little clue of age. But the intensity in her eyes contradicted her fragile appearance. She might be imprisoned in a useless body and condemned by many to reclusion and solitude; this woman was not buried alive. Against all odds, armed with a cardboard alphabet and a typewriter, Micheline had written a book in which she recounted her painful journey and talked of herself as 'a root planted in arid land.' She gave it to Marie who read it in one evening.

Thirty years earlier, Micheline had undergone an operation that had made things worse; the little movement birth had allotted her had been taken away as well as her voice. All that was left were distorted sounds and jerky, dislocated movements. Help had not always been forthcoming. Various organizations, most of them religious, had drawn back after a while; some had kept her at a distance. At first, she had embraced Christianity, but the limitations and, at times, the pettiness of those whose faith she tried to share drew her away. She turned towards Judaism, the faith of her father's ancestors, but there too she found rules and limitations she couldn't accept. God doesn't care how you worship Him, she decided; all He cares for is your love. That was the way for her. For a few months each year, she took shelter in the convent on the hill in Jerusalem. There, she found peace, generosity and understanding. There, the warmth of the sun on her face and the morning chirping of birds nourished her soul. In the country she loved, her voice took flight and became poems. One day, she gave Marie a printed collection, *Atoms of Silence*. They were intense and full of passion for life. On the back of the book, it said, 'Micheline, a bird in a cage, sings.' One of the poems was startling.

Auschwitz!

A shroud of silence

Covers the unnameable.

And from the silence springs a scream.

Here in a few words was the echo of the search that had brought her to Israel and that she had abandoned. But had she? The meeting with Ka-Tzetnik had been a dead end, but, perhaps, this didn't mean the end of her search.

Gedaliah

One day, Gedaliah remarked that if Marie had not been prey to those old patterns of guilt and unworthiness, she wouldn't have been attracted to Alex, nor would he have been attracted to her. She didn't quite understand what he meant but the words stuck in her mind and she wrote them down in her notebook.

It took her several years to understand what Gedaliah had meant: that our lives are shaped by the beliefs entrenched in our unconscious. She had lived her life convinced that she deserved abuse and punishment. For a while Alex had given her a semblance of togetherness, a sense of self-value. Once this had been taken away, her feeling of unworthiness had reappeared, stronger than ever, leaving her convinced that rejection, however painful, was all she could expect.

Jerusalem – May 1994

The heat was relentless and in front of her stretched more than two weeks of empty days. The visit to De-Nur, only four days before, might as well have happened eons ago. As for the insane encounter with the taxi driver, it had in no way allayed her grief. Curiously, though, it had barely left a trace; it was as if someone else had gone through a move which she had observed with a detachment close to indifference. The only meaningful thread in her stay in Jerusalem was her visits to Gedaliah, not enough though to fill her time.

She walked through the avenues of modern Jerusalem, had tea at the King David Hotel where the British colonial presence still lingered with the memory of the bomb which, in 1947, had killed several people in the lobby and injured hundreds of others. But everywhere she went the throbbing ache followed her. Only the familiarity of the Old City seemed to give her a semblance of relief. There, the heat was easier to escape. She strolled through the narrow lanes unreached by the sun, took refuge in churches – Armenian, Catholic, Protestant, the denomination mattered little – they all smelt of incense, candles and dust, but offered no solace. The walls polished by centuries seemed to bend towards her, suggesting that living with pain was not uncommon and that one could even get used to it. No one approached her, no one talked to her. It crossed her mind that, like animals who keep away from the weak, people instinctively recoil from the wounded as if afraid of contamination.

Marie's loneliness had taken the colour of the heat, of the slabs of stone under her feet, of the crowds that made her seek for breath, of the Russian immigrants who seemed to be everywhere begging for a few coins: in the squares, at street corners, at the terraces of the cafés and restaurants. During her previous stay, there had been none. Their outdated clothes, their skin too white, their sideburns too long were embarrassingly conspicuous even though everyone pretended they were not there. A young Russian man standing by a tree played the violin, an empty paper cup at his feet. The sad melody evoked the solitude of far off frozen steppes, not the aridity of the desert that stretched around Jerusalem. A few yards away, a woman with a faded green hat that hid half of her wrinkled face stood carrying a guitar whose strings she left untouched. From time to time, in a pathetic attempt at singing, she let out a few piercing sounds. There was no begging bowl by her side.

Later on, as Marie sat outside a café, an old Palestinian woman passed by, begging without conviction. She was dressed in the traditional black robe of her people, embroidered at the chest with bright colours. On an impulse, Marie gave her a few coins. The woman's blue eyes softened and, looking straight at Marie, she bent over and kissed her cheek. Her face, furrowed by age and hard times, was surprisingly soft, an unexpected gift.

The woman's blue eyes had brought back the memory of Ka-Tzetnik. She had never been really clear in her mind as to what she expected from their encounter. No wonder nothing much had come of it. Yet now that she was in Israel, with too much time on her hands, it appeared that she could just as well use the time and explore whatever she could gather about the Holocaust. There were libraries and people who had things to say about it. She could start with a visit to Yad Vashem, the museum of remembrance. Someone – who? – had told her that it was a place no visitor ever forgot. It was located on the outskirts of Jerusalem. She hailed a taxi which dropped her in front of the door.

Yad Vashem

The walls at the entrance were lined with the expected photographs of Nazis and their victims. Above the photographs, written in large letters, were the infamous names: Treblinka Sobibór, Majdanek, Auschwitz; twenty-seven of them. She followed a group of Israeli soldiers who were entering a dark corridor, rifles slung on their shoulders. The corridor took a sharp turn and Marie found herself in complete darkness. It took her a few seconds to adapt and notice that the space around was filled with millions of stars and galaxies, dazzling reflections of lights suspended in space, high, above, below, right, left, some far away, some close, some in clusters, all of them reflected in the infinite. Through the space, a voice rose up, at times a woman, at times a man: 'Pauline, eight years old, Czechoslovakia; Michel, four years old, France; Andrea, ten years old, Hungary...' hundreds of thousands of murdered children whose silent presence illumined the darkness. Out of the horror, a burning flame like an Eternal Sacrifice for a world in need of redemption, a sacred space where death and life met, where horror had been transmuted into awe and beauty.

Marie left shaken. If life was to have any meaning, everything, the best and the worse, had to be embraced. Nothing, absolutely nothing could be ignored.

In the days that followed, she plunged herself into books, trying to probe the depth of the tragedy that, half a century earlier, had engulfed millions in Europe. She owed it to De-Nur, she felt. Things had changed since the end of the war when few in Israel wanted to hear about what had happened. Building the future then was more important than remembering. But with the years, the question why, why evil? couldn't be repressed anymore. Yes, Auschwitz was incomprehensible but ignoring it was dangerous. There was no answer to the question, why? – any answer would be sacrilege – but not to ask the question was a betrayal. She continued her search, spent hours in libraries. In one of them, the man at the reception desk told her she should get in touch with 'the singing rabbi' and gave her a phone number.

The singing rabbi

The rabbi was staying at a hotel in the centre of Jerusalem. Room 851, Marie was told at the reception. His grandfather had been one of the very great rabbis of the time. People said at the time that his grandson had a beautiful voice. He opened the door in person. White hair, a fat belly and a big smile, he welcomed her and took her in his arms – the hug of a bear – as if they had always known each other. 'Thank you for your visit,' he said, though she was the one taking his time and should be the one to be thankful. The room was a shambles: a blanket hastily thrown on the unmade bed, piles of books everywhere, a suitcase not yet emptied or perhaps not yet filled. Jewish people, Marie thought once again, have the confidence to be themselves, unconcerned with conventions or other people's opinions. 'This is life,' they seemed to say, 'why pretend?' To add to the confusion, the room was partly filled by a group of followers who looked at the rabbi with adoring eyes. They politely kept themselves at a distance once they heard that Marie was there to interview their rabbi. He offered her a chair near the bed on which he sat facing her. At first he talked about the state of the world, about the relativity of what he called external suffering as opposed to inner suffering, which was, he said, much worse and on the increase. He offered as proof the mounting rate of suicides among the young across the world. 'So where stood the Holocaust in all that?' Marie asked.

'The Holocaust,' he said, 'is the response of God to the crisis of the world. God,' he added, 'has increased the suffering in order to be called upon. Auschwitz was not a punishment, but an education.' Marie wondered whether she understood correctly. 'God doesn't want to punish,' the rabbi continued, 'but each time Man commits a sin, that is, each time he forgets Him, God adds to his knowledge. The suffering,' said the rabbi, 'came because Man had forgotten that the reason of life is not life itself, that it is not self-preservation but the remembrance of God.' Auschwitz was His gift. The words were shocking and sounded dangerously theoretical but Marie had no argument to oppose them. The man's view on the origin of evil was built around the Talmud and the Kabbalah, of which she knew almost nothing.

She left, resolute to dismiss what she had just heard. Yet with a sentence still resonating in her ears, which she found impossible to discard: 'The Holocaust is not over. God won't tire of reminding Man.' At the door, ready to shake hands, apparently on an impulse, the rabbi said, 'I am celebrating a wedding this Thursday. Would you like to come? It will be a joyful event.' Then, turning towards a woman in the room, 'Eliah, give this lady the address.' Marie left with the piece of paper in her pocket, on which Eliah had jotted the names of a street and of a house somewhere in Jerusalem.

A Jerusalem wedding

The wedding was taking place in what looked like a large garden, part of a private estate. No one showed any surprise nor much interest at the presence there of a stranger, clearly not Jewish. The reason for the rabbi's nickname was now made clear. For the singing rabbi, accompanied by a cello and a guitar, did sing. His voice, low and rich, rose in the night to a sky teeming with stars. When, according to the tradition, the groom crushed under his foot a glass carefully wrapped in a paper bag, the crowd too burst into song. Later, Marie found herself sitting at one of the long tables lined under fir trees, a plate of lamb and vegetables in front of her. The man next to her knew neither the bride nor the groom. 'I don't either,' said Marie wondering how many of the guests happened to be here without the knowledge of the host. But in the Middle East, Marie remembered from previous travels, joy and generosity don't stand apart, particularly in the Jewish community. She and the man sitting beside her ate in silence, both keeping to themselves. After the meal, avoiding the crowd, she strolled along a path leading further on into the garden and stopped to watch a man crushing a scorpion under his foot. 'Nasty,' he said, and then walked away as if crushing a scorpion was the most normal thing in the world. But here, Marie thought, perhaps it was. She had no idea when and how she'd returned to the convent. All that was left of the evening were a series of disconnected and meaningless images that had little to do with her.

Jerusalem – May 1994

One morning, while sitting in the garden with Micheline, Marie told her that she was looking for people willing to share their thoughts about the Holocaust. Would she know of someone? Micheline immediately made a sign with her head. She seemed excited, and picking the cardboard alphabet that lay on her lap, one by one, she pointed at the letter P, then E, then R, then E... She stopped and looked at Marie enquiringly. 'Père?' Marie asked, 'You mean Père?' Micheline nodded again then started pointing at a series of other letters. Slowly she spelt the word M A R C E L. A French priest, Marie thought. Micheline continued, D U B O I S. 'Père Marcel Dubois,' Marie said aloud. The smile in Micheline's eyes confirmed that she was correct.

'Someone I should see?' Marie asked. Once again, Micheline acquiesced with a nod. As if to approve, a bird perched on a bush nearby trilled sharply. At that same moment, Sister Blandine appeared at the corner of the main house with a jug and two glasses on a tray.

'I thought you might need some refreshment,' she said as she approached, her face radiating good humour. The wide sleeves of her habit were rolled over her elbows and her cheeks had a rosy glow. She reminded Marie of one of Vermeer's women, with their calm and down-to-earth demeanour, except that here the Jerusalem light was brighter, more vivid than on the canvas of the Dutch painter.

'Who is Father Marcel Dubois?' Marie asked. The nun's face lit up. A light breeze swayed her veil and suddenly she looked like a young girl.

'Ah, Micheline told you,' she exclaimed. Marie smiled back.

'Micheline thinks I should meet him. I would like to ask him about the Holocaust.'

'This is a good idea,' Sister Blandine said as she poured the fresh lemonade in the glasses. 'Micheline is right,' she added, 'le Père Dubois has lived here in Jerusalem over thirty years and he has deep connections with the Jewish community. He certainly would have a lot to say.'

Father Dubois was a Dominican, the nun explained. He taught philosophy at the Hebrew University of Jerusalem, and was highly respected all over Israel for his unremitting work to widen the dialogue between Christians and Jews. 'He lives not far from here,' Sister Blandine went on, 'on the road just under us. His house is about three hundred metres further along. If you want, I can give you his phone number.'

Paris 2014

The Internet is such a marvel. In 1994, no one had any inkling of what it could offer. Now she types the name Father Marcel Dubois, and his whole biography appears. She discovers that he died in 2007 and that he had been born in 1920. So he was seventy-four when they met. She is surprised. He didn't look it.

She doesn't remember much of their conversation but the audio cassette is there, and like the light of a star long gone, the voice of Father Dubois reaches her from the past, as clear as if they were again sitting together in the small basement room in Jerusalem, with the birds and the muezzin echoing in the distance. They talk of the Holocaust and also of the recent massacres in Bosnia and Rwanda. Today, they would be talking about Syria and Iraq.

Jerusalem – May 1994

It was almost eleven in the morning when Marie left the Convent. A good thing Father Dubois lived so close to the Convent; the sun was beating down on the dusty road and she was already in a sweat after her short walk to his house. She rang the bell. He appeared almost immediately and opened the wrought iron gate that led into a tiny courtyard. He had an air of tranquil determination that confirmed the strong line of his jaw; his body, square and sturdy, exuded a quiet strength. The pair of brown trousers and jumper he was wearing conjured up the image of an oak tree. This man had roots that went deep. He closed the gate behind her and led her into a basement composed of one room, its walls lined with books and, almost hidden on one side, a small alcove just large enough to hold an altar and two stools. On the altar, inside a red glass, the flicker of a candle indicated the presence of the Eucharist. 'This is where I celebrate Mass when I am at home,' said Father Dubois matter-of-factly. He sat down on the sofa and she in the armchair by its side, both facing a low table on which she placed her tape recorder. 'These are mostly copies of my books,' he said as she looked at the shelves around. The sound of the birds outside only emphasized the peacefulness of the room.

For over an hour, Father Dubois shared with her his vision of the Holocaust, a vision illuminated by his Christian faith. She, who kept at a safe distance from religion, any religion, was not prepared for what this man had to say.

'If we believe that, through His Cross, Jesus conquered evil, then,' he said, *'the person suffering is either a living sacrament or, if consciously participating in the Cross, this person becomes a tabernacle where the transfiguration takes place, that is, where human nature becomes God.'*

Too moved to respond, Marie let herself absorb what she had just heard. These were incredible, shocking words, but also sacred words. They reverberated much farther than the small room where the two of them were sitting. The calmness and absence of ostentation in Father Dubois gave them even more weight. But could she accept them? Wasn't this the glorification of suffering that Christianity was so prone to? Yet this man was expressing the foundation of his faith and she could only be in awe at its depth. And although her faith in God didn't quite level to his, she was not alien to what his words implied. Years ago, the intimation of the sacredness of suffering had stirred her heart. Again she remembered the ravaged landscape with the starving Ethiopian woman, the dead child in her arms, her eyes looking far beyond this world, and then that walk through the sanitized remains of the camp in Dachau. Each time, she had been seized by an overpowering need to kneel, aware of an invisible yet tangible Presence that, she sensed, had been there all along witnessing the suffering. What Father Dubois had just said belonged to that dimension; it didn't make Auschwitz more acceptable or comprehensible – Auschwitz was as unfathomable as God – but it brought them nearer. Wasn't this what she was searching for? At that moment, the call to prayer rising from a mosque nearby echoed through the room, its sound curiously reassuring, perhaps because, ironically in a city like Jerusalem, it proclaimed to all who heard it that God had more than one voice. Father Dubois continued. *'We have to consider – this is the Christian explanation – that the Holocaust is part of the Mystery of Redemption. Such suffering,'* he went on, *'can only make sense when, through the Divine Mercy, those who suffer are saved by their suffering. But of course,'* he quickly added – the pain in his eyes visible – *'what I just said is absolutely unutterable to the Jews.'* He shifted on his seat, his hands catching for a second a ray of sun that exposed the joints thickened by time, the blue of the veins. How old was he? Marie wondered. Late sixties perhaps. She made a move. It was time to leave. Father Dubois had been more than generous with his time. He saw her to the gate and as they said their goodbyes, 'One day, Auschwitz will be remembered as Light,' he said, and then closed the gate behind her. Shaken, she stood, quivering in the heat, the priest's last words rippling in waves that, she felt, were reaching far beyond the limits of Jerusalem, Israel or even the world.

Paris 2014

After all those years, she now wonders: had not Father Dubois been mistaken in thinking that his Christian understanding of the Holocaust would have been unacceptable to his Jewish friends? Was not the Jewish author Elie Wiesel saying the same in his book *Night* about the camps when, in answer to the voice rising from the rows of prisoners and asking, 'Where is God?' someone pointed at the thrashing body of the fifteen year old dying on the gallows in front of them?

Jerusalem – May 1994

Strange how everything seemed disconnected, Marie thought. She was sitting in front of a large fountain where half a dozen children splashed each other with shrieks of pleasure. The fountain – recently built, it seemed – was decorated with three ugly bronze dolphins that spurted water. It stood in a garden facing the Old City on the other side of the valley. Half of her stay in Israel had gone by and she could hardly remember what she had done with her time. Tel Aviv and her visit to Ka-Tzetnik seemed to have happened in another life. It had led her to Yad Vashem and to several people who didn't mind sharing their views on the Holocaust, to books that explored what Father Dubois called 'the catastrophe'. Had she gained any real knowledge, any real understanding? She doubted it. All these encounters, all the books from which she had copied so many quotations, were like broken fragments of a picture that still remained blurred: her aimless walks through the city, her exchanges at the Convent with Micheline and Olivier, her vain attempts at prayer in the small chapel where, hidden from sight by a screen, the cloistered nuns sang soothing hymns; what did all these have in common? Everything felt insubstantial, as if happening to someone who was not quite her even though that someone bore her name and looked like her. Only the visits to Gedaliah gave her some sense of continuity. There, in the small office that had become familiar, they disentangled the threads of her past and brought them to the light of the present. It didn't always make much sense but, for a while, it soothed the constant ache of Alex's absence and gave her temporary relief. This was more than she could have hoped for, and she was grateful.

After each session with Gedaliah, she went and sat at the small café on the square opposite the jacaranda and there, between sips of carrot juice, she jotted down as Gedaliah had suggested what she remembered of the session. She didn't try to give it a form; she just let the confusion and the emotions pour out on the paper. She then forgot all about it and went on filling her time with her search on the Holocaust, while deep down, she knew that the task was beyond her and that no book would ever emerge from that search.

A session with Gedaliah

She is facing a high mountain. She holds something in her hands. At first, it is a black stone then it becomes a loaf of bread and finally turns into a small dead black lamb. She now climbs the mountain carrying the lamb. Though encumbered with her load, she has no intention to abandon it or to stop her ascent. She must go on and carry the lamb. As she approaches the summit, the path narrows and grows steeper. When she finally reaches the top, she finds that there is just enough space there for her to stand with the lamb that she has placed at her feet. Now she knows – she is here to offer this lamb as a sacrifice. She looks around at the view facing her; she is on top of the world and there are the continents, the seas, the mountains, the cities, all that makes this world. As if waiting for her, there is a small pyre ready to be lit and she places the lamb on it. She lights the fire; a flame springs up that can be seen from every corner of the world. Again she knows – the flame signals the Presence, and her purpose has been to make that sign visible to all. The flame rises bright and joyous; it keeps burning and will burn forever, for the sacrifice has been accepted.

Paris 2014

The words are written in tiny characters, the lines touching each other, as if the writer had been afraid of giving them too much space. She had no memory of those notes. There is so much healing here. Did that session have any impact on her? And the other sessions? She turns the pages one after the other. It becomes evident that Gedaliah was taking her through a journey, both psychological and spiritual, showing her that, however tortuous, life has a direction. Little by little, he brought to the fore the shame of the child at having missed her father's love, her guilt at having chosen her mother over him, her search for her own inner truth, her drowning into Alex's persona and the loss of whatever identity she had possessed; and all along, the Light, in which he made her bathe and become new. She was unaware of the process at the time. There were just those strange meetings with Gedaliah from which she came out a little dizzy, unable to remember much of what had happened, only knowing that for a time the pain had receded. And yet, months and years afterwards, she is convinced that without him, she might well have drowned in the despair and madness that had engulfed her. It seems strange now that for years, the notebook remained buried in a box and with it all that was related to that period of her life: the diaries, the letters, the tapes, even the contract signed in San Francisco with Alex. Perhaps because in some way, the box kept the pain at bay. To open it would have been too risky. Things had gone wrong, very wrong but she had survived. At the time, that's all that mattered. She'd had no desire to look back.

What now comes to light is that Gedaliah was presenting her with a different version of her story; at first sight, a pitiful story. But he was working at a deeper level, the only level where true healing can take place. 'My suffering is bigger than yours,' she had once mocked Alex, but life has a way of mocking you too. Hadn't she also believed that her pain was special? Not that the pain could be denied; it had been real enough but its roots were hers and after all those years, she can only laugh, though not without compassion for the woman she was.

Rummaging through the past brings to the surface memories so faint that they seem to belong to a dream. One of them, long buried, has risen. She is back in Jerusalem standing in tears on Gedaliah's doorstep on the day that she first came to him. They are still in the doorway when he mentions the name of Job. But this means little to her, which is probably why it doesn't stick to her mind. All she knows about Job is that he has lost everything, his property, his family and finally his health and that, in his despair, he calls to God, asking why He treats him so badly. But the allusion to Job is no consolation; and it doesn't occur to her to look up the Book of Job; she simply ignores the remark.

Today, after having at last a look at the Bible, she discovers that when, in his distress, filled with anger and incomprehension, Job turns to God, he demands a response. Why do I suffer when I have done nothing wrong? Why do the wicked succeed and the righteous suffer? Is God unjust? And why does God remain silent?

It seems that all of us, consciously or unconsciously, are still asking these questions, demanding meaning, demanding justice. But what Job gets instead is the vision of God in all His Majesty and Magnificence. From man's point of view, God's answer makes no sense. But what Job tells us, Marie discovers, is that when everything is lost, when everything has turned to ashes and darkness, the only response is to fall on our knees. This is the Mystery. At the core of the grief, the Eternal flame never ceases to burn and redeem. This is of course hardly acceptable and few dare say it. Yet, should we accept only good from God and none of the evil that comes to us? As she probes into the Book of Job, she hears echoes of the singing rabbi and of Father Dubois, each one in his own way saying the same thing: that the magnificence of God and the tragedy of suffering are inextricably and mysteriously bound, that the only answer to suffering resides at the core of the human being, in the soul, that most intimate place where the meeting with God takes place. From the human point of view, this is scandalous, and in that month of May 1994, the words of the rabbi and of Father Dubois were not only difficult to accept, they seemed dangerous.

Jerusalem – May 1994

Marie's stay in Israel was nearing its end. She said goodbye to Gedaliah, and for the last time, she sat at the café on the square now carpeted in purple-blue with the jacaranda's blossoms. Had that old self of hers, with its shame, its guilt, its fears, finally fallen away? She doubted but at least she had become aware of it, and now she couldn't quite forget the Light she had washed herself in, or the blazing flame on the mountaintop. And today, Gedaliah had implanted a new image, an image she found unpleasant, embarrassing even though it carried power: she standing once again on top of a mountain overlooking the world, this time, legs apart, watering the mountain, an image of fertility. She wrote it all down and closed the notebook. It was difficult to believe that these pages contained the way to her recovery. She still felt that without Alex, life was not worth living. Fear crept in; tomorrow she would be in England and London would be a desert. Of course, to some extent, her work would keep her together, and there would still be the meditation group she used to attend. With time, she would learn to live with the pain and one day, perhaps, Alex would reappear and life would start again. But right now, it seemed that nothing much had come from these last three weeks. Israel, she feared, had only been a distraction. As to writing a book on the Holocaust, this had been nothing but a delusion. She was leaving empty-handed.

Surviving – The Rumi Years

The short journey to the airport and the flight to London left no trace in her memory. She could as well have been transported in her sleep. Once back, it was as if she had never been away. She fell into the old routine of work and home, of home and work, walked through the same underground stations, climbed and went down the same escalators with their posters advertising some distant islands, the latest thriller or the latest film. Escapes, more escapes. Didn't they know that there was no escape? The image was banal but it felt true: she was a candle whose flame had been snuffed and she couldn't see any way to relight it. She made all the expected moves, did many interviews with all sorts of experts on all sorts of subjects, put together various radio programmes, attended meetings. But all along, whatever she did, wherever she went, it was as if a veil stretched between her and the world, diffusing it into insignificance. It had the advantage of keeping the pain at a distance but didn't erase it. She sometimes wondered how many people led similar empty lives, some of them with more reasons to cry than she; a thought that was no comfort. Time, they say, is the great healer but healing was unimaginable, and she couldn't believe that she, like them, would learn to live and accept the pain. And why live? She didn't see any reason for it. Yet suicide was not the answer. Death might seem like a way of escaping destiny, but destiny, she believed, does catch up. Putting an end to one's life was only avoidance. Once on the other side, one just had to come back and start all over again. No, there was no escape from pain.

London – June 1994

It was one of those sunny and warm afternoons – a Sunday – when London seems to have awoken with a smile. Marie had returned from Israel two weeks earlier, glad to fall back into her work but still with too much time left on her hands. She dreaded being alone with no task to fulfil, for then all she was left with was the gaping wound of Alex's absence.

That Sunday, the Sufi group, of which she had been a member for years, was meeting somewhere near Hampstead, not far from the tube station. Perhaps she would find some comfort there.

As she approached the hall where the meeting was taking place, she once again reflected that London, with its large spaces of green and thousands of gardens, was like no other city. Even in the poorest areas, squeezed between the dull blocks of flats, shrubs and flowers managed to bring life and colour. But this was no poor area. The avenue she was walking along was lined with cherry trees that, only a couple of weeks earlier, must have been in full blossom, and each of the large houses on both sides of the avenue had its well-cared-for front garden.

There were perhaps a hundred people in the hall when she entered, all chatting happily, and many of them nodded to her. She didn't feel like talking; it was time to take a seat. In the sudden silence, she found her mind in turmoil, thoughts rushing in from all directions. What did Alex believe? How could he think that she would say or do anything against him? Didn't he remember their time in Paris when the two of them were one?

After the opening talk of which Marie heard nothing, there was time for meditation. She couldn't stop the thoughts or her heart pounding. She could feel the blood throbbing at her temples, and she wondered whether the woman sitting beside her heard it. When would this meditation stop? Where was Alex at this moment? His heart must be pounding too; they were connected. She couldn't live without him. Around her, the silence was as deep as it was unbearable. Didn't anybody know she was being torn to pieces? At last there was a shuffling of people; the meditation was over. Time for tea and more chatting. Time for her to leave. But as she stood up, right in front of her, was Margaret, a frown on her face. With her grey wavy hair, her tweed skirts and twin sets, she looked like Miss Marple: same age – mid or late sixties – same sharp blue eyes, same unassuming appearance behind which hid an acute mind that cut through all pretence. 'Marie, what is going on?' she asked abruptly. 'You filled the room.' Her voice demanded an answer. Startled, Marie stammered out Alex's name. The question sprang. 'What did you project on to him?' 'Everything,' said Marie with tears swelling in her eyes. 'You have to re-own it,' came the answer. Margaret offered no words of solace, or pity or judgement but – how extraordinary! – in a few words, she had summed it all up. No sentimentality here, just facts. Exposed and relieved, Marie let herself cry. In the many years she had known Margaret, she had never dared approach her. It was known that Margaret had her own small group Marie would have liked to join. But though Margaret was never unfriendly, she radiated the sort of authority that kept you at a distance. It was also known that she had been a nurse but had abandoned the profession because, as she had once said, she always knew who was to die next. She confessed this was a knowledge she would have rather done without. Being clairvoyant, she often said, was not really a gift to welcome, rather an inconvenience. She had helped some well known people: Benjamin Britten when his creativity had let him down, a well known opera singer and probably many others nobody knew about. 'I am not the one who heals or helps,' she said when asked, 'I am only the vehicle.' But that day, all her attention was on Marie who, for the first time in weeks, felt that here was someone who understood. This, in itself, was a relief of some sort. She accepted a cup of tea but soon left, Margaret's concerned gaze still in her vision.

Curiously, the very next day, the heavy burden Marie had carried all those weeks and months seemed to have been lifted, if only slightly. The wound was still wide open, still bleeding, but – was it her imagination? – it didn't quite hurt as much as before. And when, three days later, at a talk given by a mutual friend, she saw Margaret again, Marie went up to her. 'What did you do?' she asked. 'I've been feeling better.'

'Hum, I have been thinking of you,' Margaret said with an uncommitted smile.

London – August 1994 – Jean

The summer was nearing its end. In the early and late hours, a new coolness in the air suggested that autumn was near. Marie kept herself busy; it was the only way to survive. As long as she did, the tearing pain of Alex's absence could be pushed aside, but she had to stay on the alert; it was still ready to insinuate itself into her life as soon as she let her guard down.

Years ago, she had heard of a woman who lived nearby and was known to help people – mostly musicians – to improve their posture as well as their breathing. Marie had been intrigued but had never felt the need to go and see her. Now it was different. Since Alex had disappeared from her life, it was as if she had stopped breathing, as if unconsciously, by holding her breath, the pain might be held at bay. Perhaps this woman could help her. She arranged an appointment. Jean lived only a ten-minute walk away.

The house stood at the corner of a quiet street near Holland Park, surrounded by a garden filled with shrubs and fruit trees. There was no bell at the entrance and no need for it as Jean didn't lock her front door. In the hall, the door to the room where the 'work' was taking place was purposely left half-open.

At first, the only things that caught the eye were plants of various sizes and shapes, all in pots, competing for the light that fell from two windows. Two large mirrors, one on the wall, the other on a pivoting frame, gave the room a liquid, almost submarine quality in which the plants seemed to float like algae. Stretched in the middle of the room, a dog lay asleep, his nose on the carpet – a rescue dog whose name was Andy, Marie was told – while, in a corner, a grand piano almost disappeared under improbable paraphernalia: a puppet elephant flopping on its legs, a series of small jars for the 'students' to leave their three pounds at the end of the 'lesson', a collection of crystals of all colours... Half hidden under the piano, a cello hinted at a past not quite gone. And, impossible to ignore, at the foot of a high massage bed, a skeleton hung from a pole a few inches above the floor. Unexpected as well as disturbing as it may have been, after a few visits it felt like an old friend. Jean used it to remind her students of their own bone structure. 'Look how the ribs are attached to the spine,' she would say, pointing at the skeleton. 'Look how the head is resting on top of the spine, not in front.' Marie looked and it was always a discovery. Why couldn't she feel it the way it obviously was; and how extraordinary that, yes, the head was 'resting' exactly as Jean was saying, 'on top of the spine'?

There were always two or three other 'students' present when Marie came in, for Jean refused to work one to one. And though the ancient wooden clock on the mantelpiece insisted on counting the hours, this didn't prevent the 'lessons' from overlapping seamlessly, as early and late comers succeeded each other with a regularity that had little to do with the clock.

Jean was in her eighties, her back, broken years ago in a sailing accident, hunched under the weight of an invisible load, her breathing obstructed by chronic asthma. Yet day after day, she gave her full attention as well as her extraordinary knowledge of the human being as if it were nothing special. She worked mostly with musicians, correcting their posture and making them aware of their body: violinists who had problems with their shoulders, pianists with their wrists. Many suffered from tendonitis. There was as much to learn from observing her as from letting her hands put pressure on your arm or your back. 'How does it feel?' Jean would ask as the student became aware of the tensions in his body, or of her shallow breathing. She seemed to have access to some well of common sense and quiet wisdom, which she never forced on anyone, but that she helped you find in yourself. Here, Marie had no doubt, was a source of nourishment not to be ignored. After that first visit, she went to see Jean every week.

Orly – October 1996

Birthdays in France don't assume the importance they have in Britain and America. To the French, a birthday is just an opportunity for the family to share a meal with, at the end, a cake decorated with candles. No cards, no large gathering of friends. Only the big birthdays, the decade ones, get more official recognition. Unfortunately, Marie's sister was celebrating her fortieth birthday. This meant that in two days, Marie had to be in Paris and meet a large number of people, family members through marriage, whom she hardly knew. Most of them would be coming from the country as only her sister lived in Paris. To them Marie could just as well have lived on the moon. A remark once made by one of them to her mother while she was present had stuck: 'My daughter is normal,' the woman had stressed, implying that living abroad and speaking another language was an eccentricity gone too far. None of them had ever asked her a question about her life in Britain or shown the least desire to visit her. Perhaps they found it threatening.

The birthday celebration would of course include the ritual refined meal, not unpleasant in itself, but lasting too long. And, her sister insisted, there would be dancing after dinner, far into the night. Marie's heart was definitely not in this, but staying away was not an option. She couldn't hurt her sister. And on top of it, there was the journey: first the train, then the ferry, and then on the other side, another train journey, a whole tedious waste of a day. In the end, Marie opted for the plane, a late morning flight that would take her to Orly. With the trips to the airports on both sides, it would take nearly as much time as the journey over land – and water – but it would be slightly more pleasant or less unpleasant, depending how you looked at it.

It was half past one when the plane landed. She was wearing the new camel hair coat she had bought a week ago on Regent Street, encouraged by her friend Shirley, who was good at making her spend money on clothes. She was still not sure whether she liked the coat or not, but in the end she didn't care. She was walking rapidly along the narrow airport corridor when, coming towards her, was Alex. No, she was not hallucinating; it was him. They passed each other; her throat suddenly tight, she called his name, 'Alex.' He stopped and both took a few steps back. His eyes, dark with fury brushed over her. Words she didn't catch were coming out of his mouth. 'I will never stop loving you,' she heard herself saying. 'Our souls can't be separated.' For a split second, his eyes softened. 'I had great affection for you,' he said. Then he was gone. For a moment, she remained immobile then mechanically, began to walk again. Why? Why did this happen? Why did they have to meet? It was as if once again she had been stabbed in the heart. She followed the arrows leading to the automatic train suspended in mid-air that took passengers to the terminal. Like a leitmotiv to the nightmare, the British Airways signature tune, a piece of classical music she knew but couldn't locate, filled the carriage; it seemed to spread a thick cloak of dread over everything.

She had managed the dinner but as the musicians arrived, Marie broke down and sobbed on her mother's shoulder. No one asked questions; her brother drove her to her cousins' flat where she was to spend the night. The next day, shivering with fever, she discovered she had the flu.

She must have gone to Orly again, boarded a plane and gone home. For she was now back in her London flat, unable to pretend, as she had done in recent weeks, that it was all a mistake, that Alex would soon phone and that everything would be just as before. Their encounter at Orly had blown away all her delusions. Alex was not to come back. The break with him had not been a bad dream from which she would one day wake up; it had happened, it couldn't be dismissed. Now she knew the reason behind their meeting at Orly. The break with Alex was a reality she had to admit... and accept.

The making of a book – a project

Marie soon recovered from the flu; it was impossible for her to pretend that the encounter at Orly had not taken place but she couldn't let go of Alex either. By now, they should have been working together on the project of the book of Rumi's quotations. This, of course, was out of the question. The letter from his publisher was clear enough. Her copy of the contract they had signed in San Francisco was still somewhere in a folder, a memento of a time when life was worth living. She had been unable to tear it off, but she now thought she could undertake the task on her own. No one could prevent her, and it would be a way of keeping a semblance of contact with Alex.

Rumi's work amounted to thousands of pages; researching and gathering the quotations would take months, not a bad way to fill the empty gaps in her life. Her decision was made. She would get on with her research, then once the quotations were collected she would set them up in order to show the successive stages of the spiritual journey, with all its pitfalls, apparent contradictions and paradoxes. After that, in a grand gesture, she would send Alex her work, and he could do whatever he wished with it.

But before all that, she couldn't ignore any longer the inner calling that was pulling at her heart, the urge to go and stand at the feet of Rumi, the poet and mystic the Turks call Mevlana. This of course meant going to Konya, the town in Anatolia where he was resting and where, all year round, pilgrims from all over the world come and pay him their respect. Somehow, it made sense. Rumi may have lived more than seven centuries ago, but before plunging into his work, it was right to have a more direct contact with him. She had no reason to resist. The scorching summer heat would be over by now, but the weather would still be pleasant; she could expect bright blue skies and warm sunny days. She bought a guide to Turkey, her tickets and booked two nights in a hotel in Istanbul. Once there, she would see how to arrange her trip to Konya.

Autumn – 1995

Rumi was not unknown at the BBC. Both the Uzbek Service and the World Service were interested in a radio programme about the man known as the founder of the Whirling Dervishes. It was agreed that Marie would collect a series of interviews in English and Turkish, from which she would put together a programme that would cover his time and his current celebrity, and would be broadcast in both languages in mid-December, when Rumi's death was commemorated. A colleague at the World Service, who had done a short programme the previous year on the Sufis in Turkey, gave Marie the address and phone number of the last descendant of Rumi. The Çelebi, as he was called – more a title than a surname – lived in Istanbul and was highly respected all over Turkey. As Rumi's descendant, Marie already knew, he was in charge of appointing the head of the Mevlevis, the Sufi order founded by Rumi's son after his father's death. This was not a negligible piece of information. That man would be able to provide her with all the necessary contacts she might need in Konya.

Istanbul – October 1995

Istanbul, the first step into the East and the last in Europe, a city in which the two worlds of Byzantium and Islam overlap, each of them filled with ghosts and splendour, each haunted by tales of murder, intrigue and massacres, and both with their symbolic monuments. To the Christians the ancient Aga Sofia that saw the coronations of the Byzantine Emperor, plus all the ancient churches and their gold mosaics; to the Muslims the grandeur of the blue mosque and the magnificence of the Topkapi Palace.

But Marie didn't really feel like a tourist. She would visit the main points of interest but her destination was Konya, the city where, seven centuries earlier, Rumi, the great Sufi poet, had taught, lived and died.

She had arrived in Istanbul the night before, and that morning she was heading to the Tourist Information Centre, right in the central tourist area of Sultanahmet. The tired-looking man sitting behind his desk looked at her with an air of resigned boredom. 'How can I help you?' he asked, suppressing a yawn.

'What is the best way to go to Konya from Istanbul?' she asked. 'Is there a quicker way than the coach?' The receptionist at her hotel had told her that the best way was the bus and that it would take her nine hours to reach Konya. Nine hours to cover a distance of some three hundred miles when it had taken her only three hours to reach Istanbul!

The man behind the desk didn't seem to have registered what she had just said, then without saying a word he sighed, picked up the phone and started an animated conversation in Turkish. Exasperated, Marie was going to leave when, to her surprise, the man handed her the receiver. 'Here is someone who can help you,' he said, adding, 'he speaks French.' Obviously, her accent had not escaped him. And yes, the man at the other end did speak fluent French. Marie explained that she wanted to go to Konya the next day and was wondering whether there was any way to reach it in less than nine hours. Also, could she book a hotel room there? The answer was rather vague though the voice was warm and friendly. He was the head of a travel agency called 'Adventure' and why didn't she come up? 'Where are you exactly?' she asked, already seeing herself wandering helplessly through a labyrinth of dark alleyways. 'Oh just round the corner. You cross the road on your left; it's right after the little café. You probably can see it from where you are.' She glanced through the pane of glass a few feet away and, indeed, a few tourists were sitting across the road drinking orange juice and coffee.

Two minutes later, she was standing in front of a small shop. Written in large black letters above the door was the word 'Adventure'. She stepped into a tiny room where two smiling girls welcomed her from behind their desks. Along the wall was a row of empty chairs but no man in sight. As she hesitated, one of the girls indicated the spiral staircase in the back of the room. She quickly climbed the stairs to find, waiting for her at the top, the man she had talked to a minute earlier. Dark hair, two deep vertical lines carved around his mouth and no moustache, he was probably in his forties. He looked tired but relaxed. 'Please, come in,' he said, making space for her to enter a small room with a traditional Turkish rug, a sofa and, in front of it, several rows of shelves filled with books and folders. 'So you want to go to Konya,' he said, making a sign towards the sofa. 'It shouldn't be difficult,' he said then turned towards a door Marie had not noticed. 'There is someone here who knows more than me. She might be able to help you.' He called a name Marie didn't catch and, a few seconds later, a young, tall Asian woman emerged from the room next door. She was wearing a dark blue skirt down to her ankles, a light transparent scarf over her T-shirt wrapped around her shoulders. Her thick black hair was pulled back in a braid. Wide brow, straight nose and a radiant skin, she was beautiful, but it was her stillness that was striking. She moved with a grace and dignity one wouldn't have expected in this run-down travel agency. She nodded a welcome.

'This lady wants to go to Konya,' the man said. 'I thought you could help her.'

The young woman nodded again and mentioned some tapes she had recently brought back from Konya. 'I am not sure they are here,' she said, 'let me see.' And she went back to the room from which she had come. Marie couldn't help herself,

'Is she Tibetan?' she asked, as if in Asia, only the people from Tibet could have such a look of nobility.

'No,' the man said, 'Mika is from Japan.' Mika came back with a smile of regret.

'I was in Konya two weeks ago,' she said, 'and I brought back some tapes. But I'm sorry, I can't find them. They are very beautiful,' she said. 'They are like meditation.' Then immediately, 'Why do you want to go to Konya?' The question took Marie by surprise. How to explain in a few words the connection she felt she had with Rumi? How to explain her desire to go to his tomb, and that curious feeling that he had taken her by the hand. 'It is Rumi,' Marie murmured. Then, holding on to the practical,

'Is there really no other way to go there than by coach?' She looked at them and suddenly became aware that these two people were lovers. Their hands couldn't help touching, their eyes couldn't help caressing each other. But there was nothing cheap or vulgar about them. They just didn't care to hide their love, not out of some exhibitionism but simply because they felt no reason to be embarrassed about it.

'Let's sit down,' said the man indicating the sofa. He sat next to her while Mika sat on the floor, her back leaning against his legs. 'Normally there are trains,' the man said, 'but at the moment, there is a strike.'

'Does it really have to take nine hours?' Marie asked. 'It's a whole day.'

'Maybe you could take an express coach to Ankara and then change to another one to Konya. That would take you only five to six hours.' And in the same breath, he added, 'So you are on a pilgrimage.'

She had not thought of her going to Konya in those terms and, again, she was taken by surprise.

'Yes, I suppose it is a sort of pilgrimage.'

Mika was looking at her with quiet attention. 'Don't worry about anything,' she said. 'The buses are comfortable and there are many hotels in Konya. You'll be all right.'

Mika's English was fluent – they were not speaking French after all – she hardly had any accent and was clearly at ease with the world. Her inner calmness, like a light, radiated through the whole room, enfolding the three of them in its warmth. What was surprising was how perfectly normal Marie felt sitting here with these two strangers. Hardly forty-eight hours had gone since she had left London and now, perhaps because most of her points of reference had been erased, it was as if she had known them for years. By now, her original questions had lost some of their urgency.

'Why don't you travel by night?' he said. 'That would save you time.'

'Yes, of course, but the next day I will be like a zombie. It's not worth it. Have you heard of the hotel Azizye?' she then asked. 'It's in my guidebook but the phone number is out of date.'

Mika didn't know a hotel by that name. As for him – she never got to know his name – it was clear that he had little knowledge of Konya. 'You'll find a hotel,' Mika said again reassuringly, 'don't worry.' Then, 'Tell us why you want to see Mevlana.' Marie knew the name meant Our Master and implied an intimacy she didn't quite feel. 'He has never been so alive,' she said, embarrassed as she felt tears coming to her eyes. This didn't escape Mika who took her hand.

'You are on a pilgrimage,' the man asserted, 'you are a holy woman.' There was no trace of mockery in the tone of his voice; he was merely stating a fact. Unable to stop her tears, Marie looked at them feeling helpless. Mika was now gently stroking her arm.

'I'm sorry,' Marie said, 'I can't help it. It is overpowering. Rumi is so alive,' she repeated.

'You are tired,' Mika said, 'too many new things.' Marie couldn't speak anymore. She let the tears run without trying to wipe them away. Was this disorientation? She didn't feel tired or afraid as Mika suggested, only a kind of emptiness which was not unpleasant. Even her embarrassment had vanished as none of them seemed to find any strangeness in the situation. She kept crying softly, her thoughts drifting as light as the breeze that moved the curtains from the open window beside her. But something in her was watching. She noticed the man putting his arm around her shoulders as if to protect her and, to her amazement, she saw herself putting her head on his shoulder. And yet at the same time, the whole scene was imbued with a sense of utter normality, stripped to its essence, each of them ignoring the usual conventions, each of them only responding to the inner demand of the moment. Marie watched the woman, exquisitely feminine, sitting at the feet of her man and stroking her arm. She looked like one of the lovers of ancient tales: Radha with Krishna, Leila with Majnun, Zuleika with Yusuf. It didn't matter that Marie knew nothing of these two people; they were the impersonal lovers of the traditional miniatures, whose love reaches far beyond them all. On her journey to the lover of lovers, as Rumi is sometimes called, it seemed that destiny had placed an image of love that was meant to impress on her her goal: the inner meeting every human soul longs for, even if unconsciously. The encounter was no accident. More like the beginning of a piece of music of which her tears and the tenderness of the moment were the first chord. 'You look like a Persian miniature,' she said to the two lovers. They smiled in response.

The thought of those who knew her crossed her mind: her friends in London, her sister in Paris, what would they say if they saw her crying quietly in the arms of two strangers in the middle of Istanbul. But this was precisely the point. Nobody here knew her. Her old identity had dropped. She had entered a dimensionless space, bewildering to the mind but home to the heart, a space where personality, nationality and even gender had no grip, and from which was surging a longing as old as the world, like a tidal wave ready to engulf her, yet not to be feared.

For a while, none of them moved. Mika curled up against the man whose arm was still around Marie. She was still crying, her head on his shoulder, the three of them suspended in a capsule of eternity.

How long did they stay like that? Marie would never know but she was the one who finally broke the spell and stood up to leave. She and Mika embraced silently. Half blinded by her tears, Marie went down the stairs and left the small travel shop in a daze, submerged by a flow of emotion she could not name. She avoided the large avenues, choosing instead the small alleyways that led back to her hotel, anxious to be alone in her room and let the turmoil take its course.

Lying on her bed, she cried helplessly for a while then the storm subsided as if nothing had happened and she started to make plans for her journey to Konya. Only then did she realize that she had not really gathered any information on how to get there or how to find a hotel. But somehow it didn't matter anymore. It seemed as if a door had opened and, that now, everything would gently unfold as it was meant to. The bus was leaving at eight the next morning. She called the reception and made arrangements for a taxi to pick her up an hour earlier.

Konya – October 1995

It was dark when the coach from Ankara stopped at its final destination. The last glimmer of a blazing sky stretching for miles over the dark plain had long disappeared, and when they pulled in, the coach was a pool of dimness enclosed in its own reflection.

The 'otogar' was the usual bustle of coaches, taxis and people, entangled in an apparent confusion, the logic of which tends to elude the Western eye. Marie headed towards a group of men standing beside their taxis, their faces barred by the inevitable dark moustache, all competing at the top of their voices for her custom. The first to approach her didn't seem better or worse than the others. She gave him her two bags and he promptly placed them in the boot of his dilapidated car. A few seconds later, they were aiming for the mysterious hotel Marie had chosen among the list of 'inexpensive' hotels provided by her guidebook. The Otel Azizye was said to be 'more expensive than most of the inexpensive ones but very nice.'

It was close to nine o'clock when the taxi at last entered a narrow lane and stopped in front of a derelict hotel announcing in red letters 'Otel Azizye'. Across the street, a few steps away, a group of young men looked at her with curiosity while she paid the taxi. The journey from Istanbul had taken her eleven hours instead of nine, due to her changing coach at Ankara. So much for the travel agent's advice! But at least the young man at the desk reassured her, yes, there were rooms available. The price? The equivalent of five pounds. She made him repeat, thinking she had not heard correctly. But yes, this was the price. When she saw the room and the shower with its taps gnawed by rust, five pounds seemed right after all.

Two narrow beds occupied most of the room but, as everywhere in Turkey, everything was meticulously clean and the mattresses were firm and smooth. Stumbling on a narrow step in the middle of the room, she went to check that the taps in the bathroom were actually functioning, only to discover that both delivered the same freezing water.

A modern-looking restaurant a few yards away from the hotel was offering the ritual meal of rice, lamb kebab and vegetables cooked in olive oil. The restaurant consisted of a large room built on two levels and violently lit with neon tubes. The few clients, a Turkish man, and a couple, obviously tourists, looked lost in the crude white light more suggestive of a hospital than a restaurant. Marie ate quickly, not inclined to linger in this sterile environment. Walking along the main street before returning to her hotel, she noticed a dozen of other hotels, all looking a lot more comfortable than her own, all, when asked, with rooms available at very low prices. She could still hear Mika's voice ringing in her ear, 'Don't worry. You'll be all right.' Why was it that Westerners always needed to be in control, and then worried about everything? For a second, Marie thought of moving to one of these hotels then decided to see to it the next morning. All she needed for the time being was a bed, and it was waiting for her. She went back to her room and fell quickly into a deep sleep to be awakened at dawn by the sound of the muezzin calling the believers to prayer. It was like the call of the soul to God, a prayer itself, reminding men of their connection with the Divine, and deeply reassuring. Still half-asleep, she got up, walked a few steps and violently stubbed her toes against the step she had stumbled upon the previous evening. Curiously, the pain didn't wake her completely and once back to bed she fell again into the same deep sleep. Two hours later, when finally awake, she discovered that the big toe of her right foot had turned black and was so swollen she couldn't wear her sandals. She put on the pair of old 'moccasins' she had brought with her in case of rain and limped down to reception.

Refusing to listen to the owner praising the high standard of his hotel, Marie went in search of another place somewhat more comfortable. Outside, the sky was as blue as on the postcards on display at the reception desk of the Otel Azizye. On the walls and the pavement, the sun filtered by the trees lining the road made bright patches of light. Impaired by her crippled toe, Marie had some difficulty negotiating her way. All along the Mevlana Caddesi, the main artery leading, as its name proclaimed, to the Mevlana Museum, most of the paving stones had been turned over. It was as if some mad archaeologist had been digging here for years, leaving behind him holes of various size and depth. She carefully walked through the chaos, each of her steps raising clouds of grey dust. There were half a dozen hotels she could book, all in various states of neglect, yet all luxurious compared with the Otel Azizye. She finally selected the one nearest to the

Mevlana Museum. Just across the street was the square that led to the Museum: a series of small ponds scattered among beds of white and red roses with, here and there, several benches inviting the visitor to rest and reflect before entering the mausoleum.

The Otel Dergah offered a modern version of the ancient caravanserai of the Middle Ages: a vast building with three floors of bedrooms set along dark endless corridors. The various rooms Marie was shown were more or less the same except for their orientation and the number of beds they contained: two, four or five, all narrow, all with clean, white sheets and a brown blanket folded at the foot. All the rooms had the same tiled shower room. There was something monastic in the simple practicality of it all, which was attractive. After all, wasn't she on a pilgrimage? The hotel was almost empty and the choice of room was hers. She chose one with two beds and a view across the street of the turquoise tiles of the 'Green Dome' under which rested the man she had come to visit. Apparently, the only time of year when it was difficult to find a room in Konya was in mid-December for the 'Wedding Night' when the city commemorated Rumi's death, a death he had welcomed as his 'wedding with eternity.'

Having settled in her new lodgings, Marie went in search of a doctor or a pharmacy; her foot was becoming more and more painful. As she passed in front of one of the numerous carpet shops set along the street, a young man with dark hair and fair skin but noticeably no moustache, emerged from the porch asking in perfect English whether he could be of help. Noticing Marie's hesitations, he quickly added, 'I am the owner if this shop, my name is Mehmet,' and he asked again, 'Can I help you?' He had an air of quiet authority which made her trust him. 'I am staying at the hotel Dergah,' she said, 'I need to see a doctor or a pharmacist. Where can I find one?' Her accent had not escaped him and he answered in French. 'There is a pharmacy a few yards away, let me take you there.' As they walked along, she explained that she had hurt her foot the previous night and feared she had broken her toe. 'We'll see,' he said calmly. 'I know the man here,' he added as they entered the small pharmacy which, indeed, was only two doors away from Mehmet's shop. Her companion started to explain her problem and, slightly embarrassed, Marie showed her foot with its dark blue toe. The man examined it for a few seconds and, shaking his head, said something in Turkish. 'Your toe is not broken,' Mehmet translated. 'You wouldn't be able to walk at all if it were. He's going to give you an ointment and in a few days you will feel better.' She bought the ointment and they walked back towards the carpet shop and her hotel. 'Can I offer you some tea?' Mehmet asked as they arrived at his shop. She visualized the little glasses of sweet steaming tea that keep appearing everywhere in Turkey, young men who seem to come from nowhere carrying them along the streets and lanes on round copper trays. She remembered the 'otogar' in Ankara and the table trolleys with their red samovar on top, which men pushed around, offering tea in exchange for a few coins. 'No, thank you. I'm first going to the Museum.' He nodded. 'Then sometime later; the shop is open until ten, ten-thirty in the evening.' She looked at him sitting relaxed on the armchair set on the pavement at the shop entrance. He was friendly, without being intrusive or obsequious. There was something reassuring about him. 'In ancient times this shop used to be a hammam,' he said. 'I'll show you when you come back.' 'Yes,' she said, 'I'll come later, after dinner.'

She walked back to her hotel; her wounded foot sending waves of pain at every step. Why did she have to injure herself on her first day in Konya? Once in her room, she massaged her toe with the ointment, picked a scarf and went out again.

It was still early. In the public garden that separated the heavy traffic of the street from the Museum, the only people were a stooped old man ambling along with a stick and a woman with her two children who were splashing each other in one of the shallow ponds. The traffic only a few yards away seemed to belong to a different world, the garden a discreet reminder that now was the time to recompose oneself before paying respect to the saint lying in state a few yards away, a clear hint too at the allegory of Sufi poetry and its intimation of the garden-paradise awaiting the lovers of God.

The carved wooden door was open. On her right, under the porch leading to the inner courtyard of the 'tekke', the ancient college where Rumi had taught and where he was now resting, a man behind a desk asked for a symbolic fee, a way of stressing that, according to the law, this was not a place of worship but of culture. Ironically, what in 1925 had been a safeguard against the meddling of the Sufi Orders in politics had recently become a protection against the pressure of the fundamentalists who would have liked to keep the 'unbelievers' at a suitable distance from the very man who welcomed everyone, whatever their religion or their lack of it. Instead, in accordance with Rumi's teaching, the Mevlana Museum was open to all without distinction of creed or no creed: Muslims or non-Muslims, believers or pagans, tourists or pilgrims, men or women. A few years earlier, following Ataturk's orders, the guards in charge of watching over the constant flow of visitors were checking that no one displayed any undue sign of devotion. But these days, the rule seemed to have relaxed and, mixed with the group of bewildered tourists, hundreds of Turkish men and women, many of them Anatolian peasants, openly prayed in the traditional Muslim fashion, hands raised open to receive the divine grace through the intermediary of one of His greatest saints.

In the inner courtyard, surrounded by beds of roses, stood the traditional fountain for the ritual ablutions, even though the place was not and had never been a mosque. Marie had been told that in memory of Rumi's death, the fountain had been called the Pool of the Wedding Night. She followed the other visitors and like them took off her shoes which she placed on one of the wooden shelves set up for the purpose near the opening to the shrine. Then, though it was not required, she covered her head with her scarf. As she walked in, she was greeted by the sound of the *'ney'*, the traditional reed pipe, a haunting sound which seemed to emanate from the walls: plaintive, obsessive, calling from the depth of time to that intimate and essential part of her. It felt as if she was being summoned and at the same time cradled in invisible arms. She stopped to look at the sarcophagi lying in rows on her right, some of Rumi's companions and followers. On her left, framed in gold, a series of texts in Arabic calligraphy was displayed, with next to them a sign written in Turkish and English supposed to be the words of Rumi: 'Come, come, whoever you are, whatever you are...' She stood there, unable to move. A vast quietness had taken over, like a memory, the memory of an infant in the arms of her mother, consoling her from some unfathomable sorrow. At last, she moved along. Only a few more steps and there, facing her, was the sarcophagus with its richly embroidered cover and on top a turban as well as the conical hat of the dervishes. There he was; the one she had come to meet.

How long did she stay there, at times leaning against the pillar behind her, at times squatting down on her heels on the floor? She couldn't tell, except that every so often she had to move her weight from one foot to the other to allay the pain of her wounded foot.

People walking around her, people turning back to look at her with unashamed curiosity. Nowhere to hide. She is exposed but she doesn't care. Silently she calls to him, aware of a power which keeps her glued to the place. Several times she thinks, this is enough, I'm leaving. Half an hour later she is still here. Her foot keeps hurting as if saying I won't let you forget me. She can't help laughing inside. There is something both absurd and amusing in this trivial reminder of her fragile body while all she wants is to forget it. She wonders: why did she have to hurt herself on the first day of her visit to Rumi?

At the feet of Mevlana

The Turks call him Mevlana, the Iranians Maulawi; it all depends
on how one interprets the Persian alphabet. It simply means Our
Master. However they call him, they come; they come as seven
centuries ago he beckoned them to. They come from the near
villages, men in dark suits with thick moustaches, their women
like round bundles with their baggy trousers and shawls
shrouding them from head to toe. They come, holding their
hands open towards him who silently, incessantly, pours his
boundless love indiscriminately on them all. They come by coach
loads from the other ends of the world: Japanese, American,
Spanish tourists...

'Come, come, whoever you are, whatever you are, come...'
Each day as Marie enters the mausoleum, the words greet her, as
alive as if they had just been spoken, reminding her of a love
untouched by time or space. 'I came,' she tells him silently. 'I
came.' She stands against the pillar, unable to keep her eyes away
from the elevated sarcophagus and its golden embroidered cloak.
She stands, mind silenced by a power which keeps everything
still and at the same time shakes the world at its core. She tries to
hold to herself – fragments of her mind blown away like pieces of
straw. Unmade, naked, she gives up. Tears roll down her face. A
woman, her head covered with the traditional scarf, looks at her,
tears in her eyes too. Unexpected accomplices, they smile at each
other, helpless: what can we do?

What is this Love she has longed for, which is now flooding
her? She has looked for it everywhere, sometimes catching a
glimpse of it, sometimes mistaking a human form for it. Except
for that secret knocking at her heart, she didn't know it was here,
that beyond the centuries Love was calling her. 'I have come; I am
here.' Who is talking? To whom? Her heart whispers to her heart,
'I have been waiting for you. At last, you've come.'

Can a heart break from finding itself? There, a few yards away,
Marie has no doubt, he is smiling. 'Have no fear,' he whispers, 'I

am your safest shelter.'

It was her second day in Konya. Like the previous morning, Marie was standing in the shrine, a few yards away from Rumi's sarcophagus, when the guard on duty made a sign, indicating she was to follow him. He was taking her outside and for a second she wondered if she had transgressed some unknown rule and was being politely expelled. The guard spoke only Turkish and only once they had reached the entrance did she understand, as he took her to a man who immediately intro-duced himself as – she didn't get the name – professor at the Seljuk University in Konya. The guard had now disappeared into the building. The professor had been looking for her, he said, and then had heard that she was in the shrine. Impossible to remain unnoticed here, Marie thought with some annoyance. The professor must have been in his forties, chubby, round-faced and friendly. He spoke good French and said that he was teaching French at the Seljuk University and could he be of help? It took Marie a few minutes to realize that by having made contact with some of the people the Çelebi had suggested, she had attracted attention.

Beside the professor stood an old man, whom she had not noticed at first. He was dressed in a grey robe and his wrinkled face expressed a mixture of seriousness and contentment. The three of them were standing in the sun outside the shrine with no shade to protect them, yet none of them seemed inclined to move elsewhere. 'I was coming here when I bumped into Haji,' explained the professor. 'Haji is a Sufi,' he went on. 'He asked me where I was going and I told him I was on my way to meet a French woman. Then Haji said that he was coming with me because he wanted to look at the heart of this French woman.' Marie was amused. This was unexpected. Could this old man really see someone else's heart? Well, she didn't mind letting him have a look; this was Konya, after all. Though sceptical, she nodded.

A few yards away, visitors kept entering and coming out of the Museum courtyard. 'Your heart is very pure,' the professor translated after an exchange in Turkish with the old man. 'He says that you will come back to Konya many, many times.' Marie was doubtful. She had no intention of returning to Konya. The old man was talking again. 'He says that in the end you will come to Islam.'

Alarmed, Marie exclaimed, 'No, no, certainly not!' The man laughed.

'He says Islam only means surrender to God.' Relieved, Marie nodded. In that case, it's all right, she thought. There was no need for interpretation and both she and the old man exchanged a smile. He then told her that this same night, she would have a dream, after which, his hand on his heart, he bowed to them and went his way.

That night, while in bed, Marie woke up at the sound of voices in the corridor outside her door. To her surprise, one of the voices seemed to be her mother's. She jumped out of bed and opened the door. There was her mother with, beside her, her brother and sister. 'You are not supposed to know we are here,' said her mother. She looked annoyed. The scene was so vivid that Marie started and, astonished, found herself still in bed. The boundaries between dream and reality had overlapped, and for a few seconds she couldn't quite disentangle them. She remembered having read that any step someone takes on the spiritual path benefits all of their close relatives. Was this what the dream was suggesting?

Paris 2014

It only occurs to her now that during all those years when she was struggling to find her way, the main thread running through her life was not Alex but Rumi. It was perhaps not surprising. After all, the book she and Alex had worked on together had been about Rumi. But it's only today, after all those years, that she's becoming aware of the depth and magnitude of her connection with Rumi and how much it had been and still is shaping her life.

Istanbul Airport – Late October 1995

Marie's flight had been delayed and there she was in this crowded airport, too small for the number of travellers Turkey attracted, with three hours in front of her and nothing to fill them. She had been told that another airport, much larger than this one, was being built. This was no consolation. For the time being, passengers had to endure the lack of seats, the running and shrieking of children, the shabby restaurant... The place was as dull as it was unpleasant.

Sitting beside her was a man absently turning the pages of his newspaper. The paper, *The Times*, Marie noticed, was from the previous day. Aware of being observed, the man turned to her. 'My plane has been delayed,' he said with a sigh. 'Has yours too?' 'Yes, three hours. Are you going to London?'

'No,' the man replied, 'I'm flying to Edinburgh and I suppose I'm lucky; my flight has only been delayed by one hour; it should be called soon.' He had a kindly face with tiny wrinkles at the corners of the eyes that said he was fond of life and not immune to a good laugh. His eyes were the colour of the sea. He could have been sixty or perhaps a bit less; difficult to say. He seemed glad to have found someone to break the boredom. 'Have you been in Turkey long?' he asked.

'Two weeks,' she said. 'And you?'

'Oh, just one week, a short escape really.' He didn't say what he had escaped from. 'This is such a different world, and yet so close; only a few hours away.' She nodded.

'Yes, I like the way things are here, less controlled. It seems a bit chaotic at first but then it's quite a relief.' He agreed with a smile.

'That's true, even though at times it can be frustrating.'

They chatted about the weather and about the carpets everywhere on offer.

'What I really would like is to go and see the villages where they are made,' she said. She added she didn't see how this could be done. 'Unfortunately, I don't know anybody who could take me.' The man sat up, suddenly attentive.

'My son-in-law sells carpets and kilims in Scotland,' he said. 'He has a shop in Edinburgh but he goes to the villages where he buys them. He could certainly give you some contacts.' Marie looked at the man, at his lack of affectation; he didn't seem to be talking for the sake of talking. At that moment, the crackling sound of a loudspeaker boomed through the building, followed by an announcement: 'The British Airways flight number 6398 to Edinburgh is now boarding,' said a female voice, first in English then in Turkish. The man stood up.

'This is my flight, at last.' Disappointed, Marie nodded. He was going to leave without giving her the details of his son-in-law. He had already picked up the worn leather bag at his feet when, taking out a pen from his pocket, 'Please,' he said, 'can you give me your phone number, I'll pass it to my son-in-law. His name is Rufus. He will call you.' He quickly scribbled the number she gave him on the crumpled *Times*, nodded a goodbye and disappeared in the crowd. Well, one never knew. Rufus – the name was unusual.

London – November 1995

Three weeks later, Marie was ready to leave for work when the phone rang. 'You met my father-in-law in Istanbul,' a man's voice said. So he had called after all. The voice was both firm and friendly. 'My name is Rufus R...' It all came back: The crowded airport, the man sitting next to her and their interrupted conversation. 'John told me you would like to go and see how the rugs are made in Turkish villages.' 'Yes, that's right, I'd love to.' 'Well,

I know someone you can trust in Konya who could help. His children and mine play together when I take them with me to Konya.' The name of the man there was Mehmet – there were it seemed a lot of Mehmets in Turkey – the name of his shop was The Silk Road. 'It is just across the Mevlana Museum, in a narrow lane by the side of the Dergah hotel,' Rufus said. 'If you tell him I sent you, he will do everything he can to help.' Marie didn't know when she would be back in Konya, but this new opening seemed like a sign; she might well go there again soon.

The autumn was more advanced in London than Turkey. There were still sunny days now and then, but here the air, definitely fresher, carried a whiff of winter. That grey afternoon, Marie was once again on her way to Jean. In spite of the cloudy sky, the walk to Jean was still enjoyable. There was little sign of life and Elgin Crescent with its blue, yellow and pink houses reminded Marie of the décor of a film. It wouldn't have been surprising to see Fred Astaire dancing on the pavement or Audrey Hepburn singing at the corner of the street. The front gardens were of the traditional kind with small lawns edged with flowery borders, except for a more daring one with semi-tropical plants that half hid a metal sculpture of indeterminate form, and another one – probably frowned upon by the neighbours – full of withered plants with a gravel path invaded by weeds. She turned left and was almost at the top of the hill where Jean's house stood when a ginger cat appeared and rubbed against her leg. She bent down to stroke him. 'Sorry! No time to have a chat.' His name was Nikoo, Jean had once told her when she'd mentioned the ginger cat. The wild bushes and fruit trees that surrounded Jean's house – more a jungle than a garden – were now in sight. Jean certainly didn't have the strength for much gardening but Marie remembered her refusing the bunch of dahlias she once had brought her. 'Flowers are not meant to be cut,' Jean had said, implying that doing so was close to a crime and that interfering with nature was wrong. Next time, Marie brought her a small azalea in a pot which she gladly accepted.

Marie walked up the four steps to the front door. She was early but time here was flexible and early or late didn't mean much. As she pushed the door open to the 'working' room, she heard Jean's voice, firm and matter-of-fact, 'Now take your violin.' She was talking to a young woman sitting beside her on one of the three wooden chairs which, with the massage bed, defined the 'work space'. As usual, Andy, the rescue dog, didn't make a move to greet her, even though the look in his eyes said that he expected some acknowledgement, like an old aristocrat welcoming his guests from the depth of his armchair, Marie thought. She stroked Andy's face and he gently let it drop on her hand as if too heavy for him. His face reminded her of the face of a deer, his eyes humid and warm and the soft creamy fur fading into a deeper brown that melted into the black of his neck.

'This is Susan,' Jean said as Marie walked in, and to Susan, 'Marie has just come back from Turkey.' Then, still addressing Susan, 'Now play your violin,' she said, quite aware of the young woman's embarrassment. Susan's fingers started to move on the strings of an invisible violin. 'Are you still breathing?'

'Oh,' sighed Susan, 'no, I was not.' She looked despondent.

'You know, playing the violin and breathing are not incompatible.' The irony was tempered by a smile. 'In fact,' Jean added, 'it usually helps to do both at the same time.' Susan laughed, shaken out of her seriousness.

'So, how was Turkey?' Jean asked as Marie sat down. She tried to sum up in a few words the experience of her last few weeks in Konya, the hours spent at Rumi's shrine, the sound of the *ney*, the smile of the woman who had dropped three cloves in her hand as a sign of friendship, the call to prayer over the city just before dawn mingling with the chorus of the birds, and more than anything, the overpowering love which had almost knocked her down at the shrine and she still felt pulsing in her heart. 'I can't quite come back,' Marie said. 'I don't know what's happening, but

I feel as if I were still there. It's not unpleasant but it makes life difficult at times. I'm awfully slow, what normally takes me an hour can take a day.'

Jean looked at her sharply. 'Ground yourself,' she exclaimed, 'you are wasting the energy; bring it back into the earth.' Her voice had an extraordinary authority. She seemed to know exactly what was happening. What did she see? Marie wondered, the energy leaking out of her? Jean caught her thoughts. 'Leave your head, think of your feet.'

Marie startled. My feet, she thought, my feet! So that's why she had hurt herself so badly on her first night in Konya. The whole scene rushed back: her limping along the dusty streets; her changing the weight on her feet while standing at the shrine to soothe the pain in her toe. Of course, she had to be made aware of her feet! The power which had made her heart pound wildly, which had brought uncontrollable tears to her eyes, needed channelling. She had not even suspected it then. That was the reason! Without the pain she would never have thought of her feet, still less of the earth. The pain had kept her grounded in spite of herself. She started laughing. 'Oh, Jean, I had to come all the way back from Turkey to understand!'

Jean smiled. 'This is no reason to stop breathing,' she said, a spark in her eyes. On the carpet, Andy stretched in happy contentment, a ray of sunshine dancing on his nose.

London – November 1995

It was time to embark on her project of Rumi's quotations. Through a friend she got access to the library of the School of Oriental and African Studies, and for days then months, she plunged into Rumi's works, the six books of his Masnavi, his lyrical odes, his quatrains, his lectures, his letters: in total, thousands of pages and almost a year of work. But how to start? She needed to follow some themes in order to pick the quotations. She thought of the seven valleys described in Attar's

Conference of the Birds, the symbolic poem that recounts the spiritual journey of thirty birds in search of their king. But she couldn't find any quotation in Rumi's work that fitted Attar's themes. This was like searching for the famous needle in the haystack. She decided to go the other way round. She would pick whichever lines or verses attracted her and then see if any themes emerged from her picking. This was not very logical nor was it the method a scholar would have adopted but scholarship had little to do with Rumi's message.

She spent many quiet hours in the library at SOAS, immersed in Rumi's works. She walked the streets, did her shopping, cooked her meals, all along filled with his words. It was as if he was constantly at her side whispering words that spoke to her heart, sustained and reassured her. As she turned the pages of one of the books piled in front of her, a verse would catch her eyes: *'Do not grieve when losing what escapes you, this misfortune deters great misfortunes.'* No, there was no need for using logic or scholarship in collecting these quotations; in fact it was impossible. They came to her of their own accord. In Paris she'd had the awful presentiment that one day there would be an end to her work with Alex. She remembered the promise she had then been given, *'There will be more and more joy.'* At the time, she didn't want to hear this; but now, through his Masnavi, Rumi was sending her a similar message: *'Sorrow chases away the withered leaves in the heart then new green leaves can grow; sorrow uproots the previous joy then a new delight springs from beyond.'* Would that ever be true? She was not sure. But she could not deny that this constant walking with Rumi was giving her a sense of peace and nourishment.

It was the beginning of winter when she received an intriguing letter signed Mustafa, a Turkish psychiatrist who lived in the south of Turkey. The letter, written in perfect English, mentioned the Çelebi who had given him her address. Mustafa would be in

London with his family sometime in the coming months, he said, hoping Marie would agree to meet him. Before that, he suggested she contact a close friend of his, a man called Kayan who lived in London and whose details he included in the letter.

Kayan, Marie discovered, worked for the judicial courts as an interpreter for his compatriots, when they happened to find themselves at odds with British law. He was also deeply involved with the work of the Mevlevi Order. Marie and he exchanged a few letters and it was finally agreed that on a certain evening at the end of January, she would meet Kayan and Mustafa at the address he gave her, somewhere in Mayfair.

January 1996

It was approaching eight o'clock when Marie pressed the bell at the door of a small block of flats just behind Park Lane, one of the wealthiest areas in London. The cold winter wind was sweeping through the night, scattering the rare snowflakes that braved the freezing temperature. She pulled up her collar, and was tightening her scarf when the door opened. The man standing there introduced himself as Kayan. Tall, wide shouldered, with dark hair, he looked exactly as she had imagined him; his dark blue suit and tie reflecting the same formality as his letters, the expression on his face both severe, yet welcoming. 'Please come in,' he said as he led her into a large room, which at first she thought empty. On second look, Marie noticed four chairs against the wall and a table that had been pushed into a corner. Then a man entered from the other side of the room. He too wore a suit but the shirt and tie were replaced by a white turtleneck, which gave him an air of casual elegance. 'Thank you for coming tonight,' he said. 'I am Mustafa; I wrote to you from Bodrum where I live. I am glad we meet at last. Please sit down,' he added as he pulled one of the chairs away from the wall, offering it to Marie. Once she had sat down, each of the men picked a chair and they both sat in front of her a few feet away. They looked solemn. Was this a test? Was this an interrogation of some sort? Mustafa was the first to speak. 'We are planning to organize an international meeting next spring in Turkey with all the people involved with Mevlana, Rumi,' he corrected himself. 'Which is why we've asked you to come here tonight. But,' he went on, 'we want to know how you came to him.'

'This is a long story,' she said, thinking of Alex and how in some way because of him, she had ended up in Konya. But Mustafa was unconcerned, 'We have all night,' he said quietly. 'Listening to your story is why we are here.' This was not politeness. The man meant what he said.

And so Marie poured out her story: the meeting with Alex, their working together on a book dedicated to Rumi's life and his teaching, the extraordinary osmosis between them, 'between our souls,' she said. And then the sudden break and her collapse into an abyss of pain. Her voice resounded against the silence of the two men whose faces showed an acceptance and a lack of judgement she had not expected but found soothing. They were both listening intently, asking no questions, one of them only nodding from time to time as if to say, 'I understand.' Marie talked of her visit to Konya, of the overwhelming power that had shaken her. As she went on, the room as well as time seemed to be expanding. Mustafa had stressed the night was theirs. There was no pressure. The words flowed with the same inevitability as a river running its course. She mentioned her project of a book of quotations of Rumi, 'almost finished,' she said. Then she stopped. There was no more to tell, and as if on cue, a woman entered with a jug of fruit juice, four glasses and two plates of sweets on a tray.

'This is Dina, my wife,' Mustafa said as he and Kayan stood up, and to Dina, 'This is Marie who might soon join us in Turkey.' So she had apparently passed the test. The two women smiled at each other while Dina placed the tray on the table. They sat down and chatted for a while. There was something unreal in this meeting with strangers in the middle of the night, and yet it now felt as if Marie had known them for a long time, perhaps because just a minute ago she had shared with them some of the most intimate moments of her life. Dina was from Switzerland.

'Living in Turkey is not always easy,' she said. 'Nothing works there, but the compensation is that everybody helps each other.'

'This is true,' Mustafa agreed. 'I too get frustrated at times, but people in Turkey have big hearts.'

It was close to midnight when Marie finally left. Both Kayan and Mustafa took her to the door. The wind rushed in when Kayan opened it. They didn't shake hands. She took a few steps in the cold then impulsively looked back. Kayan and Mustafa were still in the doorway, both bowing to her, their hands on their hearts.

Two weeks later, she received the official invitation to an international retreat. It was to take place at the end of May in Bodrum, a small town on the Mediterranean coast in the south of Turkey, where, as he had said, Mustafa had his home.

In the meantime, Marie would attend the weekly meetings Kayan offered in his home near Canary Wharf, the new modern London that, for the last decade, had been rising steadily in the east of the city. There, in Kayan's flat, overlooking the Thames, some seven or eight people met regularly to pray and chant a series of invocations in Arabic; after which they shared tea, cakes, fruit and friendship. The place radiated warmth and friendliness, but except for Marie and a young Englishman these people were all Turkish. They were certainly sincere, Marie had no doubt about it, but addressing God in Arabic was not for her. She would never be able to pray in a language that was alien to her, part of a different culture. And yet she enjoyed their company and the more she got to know Kayan, the more she felt affection for him.

The making of the book

She had collected hundreds of quotations. She had been right; themes appeared that she began to arrange in a meaningful order. Soon she would be able to send the whole lot to Alex. Jean as well as her friends disagreed. 'This is your work,' they all said. 'You must publish it. It would be absurd to give it away.' Marie hesitated then finally admitted they had a point, and also that the idea of making contact with Alex filled her with dread. How would he react? She didn't even know whether he would accept her offer. He might reject it and how would she feel then?

The structure of the book was now well defined; it had sixteen chapters starting with the very first step of the quest and finishing with the annihilation in God beyond death, the goal of the Sufi.

One day as Marie was discussing the book with Kayan, he suggested that the head of the Mevlevi would be happy to write a foreword. Kayan would translate it from Turkish into English. The offer was as unexpected as it was exciting. The book would have the seal of Rumi's lineage. Marie was more than grateful; the book, it felt, was blessed.

But when the time came to find a publisher, she got nowhere. Here was a book offering some three hundred quotations by Rumi, but the person who had compiled them was unknown and had no scholarly credentials. In Britain as in the US no one was willing to take the risk. All that work for nothing! Her friend Robbie suggested she, at least, find another use for her work. 'Why not write a play using the quotations,' she said. 'It's such a shame to leave all this work in a drawer.' The idea felt preposterous. Marie had never written a play, and even if she did, what to do next? Yet in spite of herself, the idea grew. Rumi's work was becoming well known in so-called spiritual circles. Readings of extracts of his poems were taking place in various venues, often with musical accompaniment. But there was never any context. It was as if Rumi's work had been born out of nowhere. Ignored was his encounter with Shams, the mysterious dervish who had come all the way from Iran to meet him. Ignored was his grief at the brutal disappearance of the man who had opened to him a direct path to God. It seemed somehow unsatisfactory to make Rumi's work known without showing how it had come to be. It was Alex who had introduced Marie to the story behind Rumi's work: the encounter with Shams followed by his disappearance. This was at the core of Rumi's transformation from the respected religious teacher that he was, into the poet and mystic whose work still moves the hearts of men. How could this be ignored? Indeed it made sense to share Rumi's story, not in the way Alex had done it, that is, with his own fiery temperament, but in letting Rumi tell his story through his own words. Yes, perhaps she should give the idea a try. This was a new challenge but challenges had a way of sustaining her.

Winter 1997

'How are you doing?' Jean asked Marie one day. 'The book is finished,' she said, 'but I can't find a publisher though I tried every possible route, England as well as America.' She was going to mention Robbie's idea of making a play out of the quotations when Jean said calmly, 'Well, I'll give you the money, and you do it yourself.' Marie was astonished. This was totally unexpected. Startled, she saw Jean picking up her chequebook from the bag she always kept at hand and writing a large cheque, which – Jean made clear – Marie had no choice but to accept.

This was another challenge. How does one produce a book? Well, just go step by step, she told herself. The first step consisted in finding out which basic rules to follow. She browsed through the bookshops in search of a guide that would take her by the hand. And there it was, a small volume less than two hundred pages that went carefully through each step, explaining in detail how to design and produce a book: choosing the right font for the text, setting it up on the page, reading galley proofs, marking the corrections. The book was invaluable. Then there was the choice of an illustration for the front cover and the writing of blurbs for the back cover and finally finding a printer. One of the publishers Marie had been in contact with suggested one in Malta. 'Their work is of a high quality and they are cheaper than the ones in Britain,' she was told. Interprint confirmed that they would be happy to work on Marie's project and yes, the price was significantly lower than the ones she had been quoted in Britain. It took Marie eight months, dozens of mock copies and numerous exchanges of letters for the book to be ready for printing.

Summer 1997 – Malta

It was June 1997 when Marie flew to Malta for a last check before the actual printing took place. She brought with her the colour sheets of the photographs for the cover. At the airport, two stocky men with dark hair and smiling faces – the head of the printing company and his assistant – were waiting for her. The heat was intense, and as they drove, the dry white stone walls of Malta seemed to vibrate in the blinding light, still exacerbated by a surprising absence of trees. They dropped her at her hotel and picked her up for dinner. They were kind, traditional men, proud of their island and of its history, particularly during the Second World War when, between 1940 and 1942, Malta due to its strategic position became one of the most bombed places in the world. They told her how the Allied convoys braved the German torpedoes and how few of them succeeded in bringing supply and reinforcement to an island close to starvation.

The next day, after a tour of the printing premises, they went through the last details before printing: deciding which font to choose for the lettering on the cover, the exact place of a small diagram on a paragraph, the choice of frame around the rose illustrating the chapter on Love. In between, Marie managed some sightseeing with a tour of Valletta and its churches; a visit to an open air museum filled with gigantic prehistoric goddesses carved in crumbling ochre stone and dating back some seven thousand years. More importantly, she arranged to meet and interview the two historians she had contacted from London for a radio programme. She was even able to take some refreshing dips in the sea. When, after only four days, she boarded her flight back to London, Marie had a sense of mission accomplished. Everything had gone smoothly and in a few weeks, the book of Rumi's quotations would be ready.

The plane was approaching the coast of England, when on the Tannoy, the pilot's voice announced that they were going to have an emergency landing. 'We are currently running on two engines only,' he said. Through the window, the right wing appeared to carry two engines. Which of the two had stopped? It could be one on each wing or two on one wing. The pilot didn't elaborate. What seemed clear was that the plane was now running on half its power. 'We will be landing at Gatwick instead of Heathrow as originally planned,' the voice further announced. The stewards were checking that bags, books, papers, everything that could move, were placed under the seats; they then began to dismantle the partition between economy and first class. Except for the screams of a baby and the sound of the engines – the two still functioning – the cabin had fallen silent, the line between life and death suddenly too thin to leave room for any comment. As the plane began its descent, it crossed Marie's mind that in Malta the printing had already begun and that if the plane were to crash, the printer would never get his money. She felt sorry for them. But there was nothing she could do about it. Outside, the patterns of green fields were speeding towards her; inside, the baby's screams filled the space. It must be sensing its mother's fear, Marie thought. She closed her eyes. They were approaching the runway, and, waiting for the crash, she bent down in the prescribed position. She didn't feel much fear, just a little squeezing in the stomach. The minutes turned to seconds that felt like hours, then a bumpy landing and the plane ran safely on the tarmac until it stopped. Half a dozen fire engines were surrounding the plane and, in the cabin, the passengers' cries of relief were muffling the baby's screams. A moment later in the airport, they looked at each other with shaken smiles. 'Sister, did you pray?' a woman asked the nun who happened to be among them.' 'Of course, I prayed, of course.' Her face radiated a confidence in God most of them were likely to lack. For her part, Marie had forgotten to pray or call to Rumi; she had only worried about her book and its printing. Well, she was now reassured, the printer wouldn't have worked in vain.

The book – two thousand copies – arrived in London a month later. Marie gave one to Jean who admired it then put it on a shelf and never looked at it again. She admitted she didn't care much for Rumi; 'too much of a whimper,' she said. Her remark made Marie laugh. She loved this woman and it didn't matter whether Jean cared or not for Rumi. Jean's aim had been to rekindle some self-esteem in Marie while keeping her busy and somehow, she had succeeded. Marie was beginning to have a sense of a self free from Alex. One day, Jean remarked, 'You're getting free of your shackles.' Marie didn't quite understand what she meant, but she noticed that her breathing had improved.

She found a distributor to store the books and sell them in both the British and the American markets. It sold well. Four hundred copies the first month, which, Marie considered, for a book that'd had no backing was not bad.

Bodrum – May/June 1997

The forty or so people gathered on Mustafa's property had come to Bodrum from a variety of countries. There were of course several Turks, some of them like Kayan had come from England, Nader was from Tabriz in Iran. Others had come from Switzerland, the Netherlands, the States and even Chile. Marie was the only French guest but that didn't count, she thought, as she lived in England.

The idea behind the gathering was to bring together a group of people who, in some way, would protect the name of Rumi and prevent his teaching from getting distorted or misused. Praiseworthy but probably naive. The surroundings were idyllic: three main buildings disseminated through an orange grove where a few peacocks, unbothered by the invasion of their territory, roamed freely, and where, under a period of one week, all the people assembled here were to live together in an atmosphere Marie could only describe as love, though no word could really convey the mixture of friendly enjoyment, generosity, shared devotion and lightness that filled the place; a parenthesis in the competitive and bustling world they had all left behind. Here, apart from having to get up at four every morning, life flowed without any constraint. There were times of prayer and meditation as well as periods spent immersed in Rumi's teaching, but there was ample time for conversation, a nap or a refreshing swim in Mustafa's pool, as the Turkish sun was unforgiving. Presiding over the retreat was a man of small stature in his late fifties, the head of the Mevlevi. His dark eyes looked at you as if saying, don't worry, you are more than safe with us, you are loved. And this felt true; love so absent from the grind of modern life, or worse, sugary and fake. Here it was alive, its power almost overwhelming.

On their last day a surprise was in store. To begin with, a treat they all welcomed, from four o'clock, waking time was moved to seven. There would be an excursion they were told after meditation and breakfast. They all embarked on a coach with no idea of destination. Ten minutes later, they were at the harbour facing the ship that was waiting for them. It was one of those large wooden barges, especially equipped for touring the coast with, on board, a crew in charge of the traditional kebab lunch. They boarded, as excited as a bunch of schoolchildren on a day out. There was nothing to do but lie on the deck in the sun, enjoy each other's company and admire the scenery: the blue of the sea, the shimmering outline of a small island in the distance, the harbour moving away. The scene carried a feeling of serenity and peace enhanced by the cries of the gulls. It felt like a reflection of the atmosphere they had shared all week. Later on, the boat stopped in the open sea to allow for a swim. Lunch consisted of the expected lamb kebabs with fresh cucumbers and tomatoes. They were good and they all ate with appetite. At the end of the day, as the heat began to recede, the Teacher talked about Mevlana and the abundance of his love, which, he said, was not only for a few but for everyone ready to receive it. How strange, Marie thought: the love pouring from Rumi and the loss of Alex had the same intensity and they seemed to mingle. It all felt like a gift, a gift that was beyond her understanding. But there was no need to understand nor was there any shame at crying and being oneself. This, too, was a gift.

They came back to Mustafa's home, drunk from the sun and fresh air, their skin salty and smelling of the sea. Everybody was leaving the next morning; it was time to pack. Some in the group had arranged a three-day stay in Konya before going back to Istanbul to catch their planes back home. Marie decided to join them. She remembered the old man telling her she would come back to Konya many times. She had not believed him then.

Konya – June 1997

Night was falling when they arrived in Konya. Suspended over the Green Dome, a full moon flooded the city with silver. They were all tired and, apart from Marie, they all had already made arrangements for their accommodation. 'What about you?' asked Nader, the Iranian man who was part of the group, feeling it his duty to protect the only woman among them. Marie nodded towards the Dergah hotel across the road. 'This is where I am staying,' she said, without saying that she hadn't made a booking. Mika's word still rang in her ear: 'Don't worry, you'll be all right,' she had said and, as promised, everything had gone smoothly. 'See you tomorrow morning, nine-thirty,' said Ben, the American who had his entrées in Konya and as such had become the leader of the group, 'at the door of the Mevlana Museum,' he specified. She nodded and crossed the street to her hotel.

The man at the reception had a familiar face though his name escaped her. He welcomed her with a large smile half hidden under his thick moustache. 'Good to see you,' he said as if she had only been away a few days. She smiled back, glad to be made to feel that she was no ordinary tourist, though the man was probably as welcoming to any customer who came more than once to the Dergah. 'I'm glad to be here again,' she replied. She chose a room similar to the one she'd had the year before; it was perhaps the same. Tomorrow, she would have to find a way to leave the group and go in search of Rufus' friend and his shop. Right now, a bed was the only thing she could think about.

The following morning stretched forever. After meeting as planned at the Museum, and a short visit to Rumi's mausoleum, the group was taken by bus to a pompous building where they were led into a vast panelled room. There, three formally dressed men greeted them, one of them gesturing towards four large sofas that almost filled the room. Two youths had appeared with glasses of tea. After an exchange of polite smiles, one of the officials – Konya's mayor, Nader whispered in Marie's ear – made a welcome speech, to which Ben responded with another speech, thanking the mayor for his hospitality. The ceremony over, everybody got up to leave. Marie thought they were now free. But no! The bus waiting for them at the door was now on its way to the museum of prehistoric artefacts where a visit had been especially organized for them. The guide explained that most of the objects they were to see came from Çatal Hüyük, a Neolithic site south-east of Konya where recent excavations indicated that a city had existed there some five thousand years ago. Marie remembered the various carpet dealers who claimed that the patterns decorating their rugs were the same as those found on murals recently discovered at the site; proof, they said, that the weaving of carpets had its roots deep into the past. True, the patterns she was looking at were the same as those she had seen on the carpets; but that didn't prove that the people who lived there some 9,000 years ago were weaving carpets.

Finally the visit was over and they were driven back to the Mevlana Museum. Marie couldn't join the others for lunch, she was to meet a friend, she said. Well this was almost true. She would meet them later in the day. She left the group and went in search of the shop Rufus had mentioned.

She had only walked a few yards along the lane adjoining the Dergah hotel when she saw, hanging over a door, the sign with the words The Silk Road. In the window, scattered over a threadbare kilim, several artefacts were displayed that, if one were to judge from the layer of dust covering them, must have been abandoned there a long time ago: a stoneware jug, three engraved metal plates and two candelabras. The old man sitting on a chair beside the open door and drawing on his cigarette paid no attention to her when she stepped in. For a few seconds, she stood blinking in the dimness until she discerned the carpets piled against the walls, which were decorated with kilims. The square room she was standing in consisted for the most part of a platform with, in a corner, a small recess with a desk covered with papers. Two men were sitting on the banquette that ran along the far off wall of the platform. In front of them was a small round table with two empty glasses. One of the men had stood up.

'Good morning, Madam. Can we offer you a glass of tea?' He made a gesture inviting Marie to walk up the three wooden steps towards them. Well built, with a square face and brown eyes that were not exactly inquisitive but very alert, there was something a bit rough about him. He exuded strength and confidence and had none of the obsequious servility of many of the other shopkeepers. A man with large wings, Marie thought, the kind of man one feels secure with. This must be Mehmet.

'I… your friend Rufus told me about you,' she began. It was as if a curtain had been lifted. All of a sudden, the man's expression had changed. He was even more alive and while his body appeared to straighten, his eyes narrowed and he looked at her with new intent. No doubt she was being weighed up. He was quick to make up his mind and soon relaxed. From prospective customer, she had become a friend. 'My name is Marie,' she said, 'and you must be Mehmet.' He smiled the smile of a child, happy to be acknowledged.

'Please, please do sit down, you are most welcome.' He turned towards the other man who had also stood up, 'This is my brother, Muammer.' Muammer looked younger than his brother, and more sensitive; there was a kind of gentleness about him that was lacking in Mehmet. Marie could tell from the way he looked at her, straight in the eyes as he shook her hand, that he was just as confident as Mehmet but more reserved. Until then, he had remained silent.

'You are very welcome,' he said. 'Please do sit down.' He spoke English well. Marie sat down on the banquette beside him, feeling curiously at home. 'Muammer,' said Mehmet, 'does business in Fethiye. I have another shop there; it's only open in the summer; he is going back the day after tomorrow.' Fethiye, Marie had read in her guidebook, was a coastal resort, a tourist haven, the kind she would rather avoid. At that moment, a couple came in and stood, hesitant, in the doorway. Mehmet was already standing. 'What can I do for you? Please come in.'

Marie observed the two brothers in action: first a welcome followed by an offer of tea then light chit-chat. It was like a ballet. The couple were from New Zealand, yes they wouldn't mind looking at a few carpets, no, they didn't want tea. They sat down on the banquette beside Marie, and Muammer began to pull the carpets one after another from one of the piles. The woman was shaking her head, 'No, I don't like this one.' Her husband disagreed, 'The colours are wonderful and the size is right.' His wife still shook her head. Muammer pulled out another carpet and Mehmet did the talking: 'This one comes from eastern Turkey, this design, very ancient, from prehistoric times.' The couple were not interested and Çatal Hüyük was not mentioned. 'The colours are all natural dyes,' he said, 'you can tell if you pass a wet rag on it. You see,' he said rubbing the rug with a wet piece of cloth. Half an hour went, dozens of carpets were spread, prices were mentioned. The face of the man betrayed nothing but his wife kept shaking her head. Finally, they stood up. 'We're not sure, we need to think,' the man said apologetically. The woman was already at the door. Muammer began to fold back the carpets. 'Perhaps they come back, perhaps not,' said Mehmet. 'Tourists,' he shrugged with a laugh. 'They want cheap stuff. Cheap I don't have. It doesn't matter,' he added, 'my clients are in Japan, in America. They come once or twice a year and they buy a whole stock.' He turned to his brother. 'Now let's have lunch.' 'You hungry, yes?' Marie nodded. It was hardly a question and refusing would have been unfriendly; anyway she was hungry. From the restaurant across the lane came kebabs and flat bread and salad. Muammer produced the plates and paper napkins. As they ate, Mehmet talked about his house. 'My mother and sisters, they grow all our food. You must come; I'll show you.' Again, this big laugh of his, full of childlike pride. Marie could have stayed here all day. But she was supposed to join the group; there were a few other semi-official meetings to attend.

On the second day of their visit, Marie was surprised to find the professor at the Seljuk University among the officials. The professor didn't speak English, the language that was being used; this time it was Marie's turn to interpret for him in French. She was beginning to miss her independence. Once again, she felt trapped, surrounded by people whose interests she didn't quite share. If she didn't escape, she might suddenly burst into tears and run out of the room. Pretending to be ill – this was not far from the truth – she fled to Mehmet's shop. There, among the piles of rugs and kilims a glass of tea in front of her, she felt free again watching the customers and the carpets being displayed. She tried to guess which customer intended to buy and which one was merely filling time. She was not always right.

It was her last day before the group was to leave Konya. She finally mentioned her desire to go to the villages and watch the carpet being woven. 'Rufus told me you might help.' Mehmet's face lit up. 'That's easy, but now is not the right time. You must come back next month when I go and buy the wool. Then you come with me.' He took a sip at his tea and added, 'I only buy spring wool; it's the best, the one that has grown during the winter.' This was business; this was what he was good at. He became excited. A boy appeared at the door not sure whether he was welcome or not. Mehmet gave him a quick glance and clapped, 'Yes, Ali, tea for the lady and for me.' The boy disappeared. Mehmet leant against the wall. 'You come with me when I buy the wool and then afterwards, you see how it becomes a carpet. First we wash the wool, then there is spinning, then I dye it and finally the weaving, and...' he paused. His eyes had softened; he seemed to be looking far into the distance. 'I take you to my village in the Taurus Mountains. It's beautiful.' His voice was full of passion. This was exactly what she'd hoped for.

'That would be wonderful,' she said. 'You tell me which date is right for you and I come.' Amused, she noticed that unconsciously she was adapting her English to Mehmet's. She wondered how he had begun to be involved in the carpet trade. It couldn't have been easy.

As if responding to her silent question, 'You know how I started my business?' he asked without waiting for a reply. 'I was fourteen when I first came to Konya. I had nothing; I sold vegetables in the streets. I was a nobody, a village boy. People looked down at me.' His jaw suddenly tight signalled that the anger and the hurt had not gone. 'I was going to show them. I had a friend, and together – I was seventeen then – we bought one rug and we sold it. Yes, this is how I began. Then we bought two carpets, then a few more.' He stopped as Ali was back with two glasses of tea on a tray. The boy put them down on the small table in front of them, picked up Mehmet's empty glass and disappeared again. Mehmet cleared his voice. 'The other carpet sellers,' he said, 'they are like dynasties. Their families, they have lived in Konya for years and years. They... how do you say... they despise village boys. But now, see.' He looked round, at the piles of rugs, at the walls clad with more rugs and kilims. 'I have customers all over the world, in America, in England, in Japan, the Netherlands. And you know,' he went on, 'I pay the women the right price for the weaving. These people are poor; I don't take advantage.' He beamed with pride and why not? He had come all the way from his village with only a basic education; he'd had to learn English, to deal with banks, customs, exchange rates, and of course, he'd had to learn about wool, dyes. He'd gone as far as India to buy some of these dyes, he said. 'I never use chemical dyes.' It was difficult to disentangle the boasting from the truth. Whatever, the man was impressive. She picked up her glass – the tea strong and sweet – and glanced at her watch. She jumped. She had been here for almost two hours. The Bodrum group had been invited by the director of the Mevlana Museum; she was supposed to be there in five minutes. No time to change and refresh. She would go the way she was, hair in a mess, skirt creased. 'I have to go,' she said. 'I'm sorry. I'll come back tomorrow morning before I leave.' Mehmet nodded. 'No problem. See you tomorrow.' As she passed the door, she turned back. 'I want to go to your village,' she said as if she feared he would forget or change his mind. This time he only waved, still smiling.

Konya – July 1997 – The wool

It was mid-July when Marie returned to Konya, hardly six weeks since her last visit. This time she came through Antalya, the Mediterranean city where, at the time of Rumi, the Seljuk Sultans spent their summers. The flight, direct from London, landed in the evening. This meant spending the night in Antalya and catching the bus to Konya the next morning before the heat became too intense. Antalya was not a closer route to Konya than Istanbul for there was no motorway and, in the end, the drive took barely less time. But the scenery was a lot more picturesque. Before reaching the sun-beaten plain of Konya, the coach had to take a steep and winding road and climb through forests of pines clinging to red earth ravines. It was magnificent and as the temperature dropped, the air became cooler.

It was late afternoon when they arrived at their destination. A short drive from the otogar to the Dergah hotel and here she was, as if she had never left. 'You, good customer,' said the man at the reception who gave her a discount in acknowledgement of her loyalty. And picking up her suitcase, he took her to the same room on the first floor that she'd had last time. There, were the two beds next to each other, each with its carefully folded brown blanket on top, which, at this time of year, she was certainly not going to need. In the left corner of the bathroom, the broken tile had not been replaced. 'Welcome to Konya,' grinned the man as he left the room then closed the door. She stretched, glad to be back in the familiar surroundings. She was always surprised at the way a few hours on a plane could so easily turn the life left behind into a faint memory, and even make bearable the thought of Alex or rather his absence.

She quickly emptied her suitcase: a few light summer clothes, some underwear and an extra pair of sandals; that was all she needed here. Then she went downstairs, smiled at the man at the reception and crossed the road to the square in front of the Museum. First, to pay her respect to Mevlana, then she would go and see Mehmet.

The sound of the *ney* enfolded her as she entered the mausoleum with a flow of Turkish peasants. As last time, her back against the pillar, she stood behind the crowd facing the sarcophagus and closed her eyes, relieved at being at last fed with this love energy, which, curiously, she had not been aware of missing. It was like getting a glass of water when you didn't even know you were thirsty, and suddenly realizing that this vague uneasiness you had been feeling for so long actually was thirst.

It was night when she left the shrine but she didn't fear missing Mehmet. It was early enough and anyway, he didn't close the shop before ten or ten-thirty. She had not told him the exact day she planned to arrive, but he knew she was coming this week. She crossed the road and went straight into the lane that led to the shop. As she came near, she saw the shop was lit and the door open.

July 1997

They were to leave at 5.45 before the heat started to crush them. Like every morning, Marie had been awakened by the call to prayer announcing that dawn was not far off. It was like a series of echoes coming from every direction, filling every corner of the sky, some distant, some that seemed to rise from the hotel itself. They mingled with the chirping of the birds, like hundreds of voices sending their longing to Him and at the same time making His silent Presence all the more tangible. This time, instead of sinking back into sleep, secure in the knowledge that people out there were praying, she got out of bed. Mehmet was to pick her up downstairs in half an hour. She had just enough time to get ready.

The sky was turning pink as they hit the road. Soon the sun emerged, soaking up the coolness of the night. After an hour, they left the tarmac road for a dirt one, leaving clouds of reddish dust behind them. They stopped in a mountain village that clung to a steep slope, where Mehmet thought he had left a scale. The scale was not found but after a breakfast of yoghourt and bread, the mayor, a grey-haired man wearing a cap, a purple shirt and a woollen sweater, decided to join them. He nodded at Marie and sat in the back of the car where he remained silent. Apparently undisturbed by the heat, he kept his woollen jacket on. They finally stopped in a small town bustling with people. By now it was past seven. It was here, said Mehmet, where he was to buy his wool. All the villages around brought their wool, freshly shorn, to this town.

The wool market was only a few yards away, set on a large square already bustling with people. Some of them had come on carts pulled by horses, others in small vans loaded with massive bundles of greyish wool. They were all busy arguing, bargaining, with wads of dirty bank notes passing from hand to hand. The smell of sheep mixed with cigarette smoke. Young boys kept emerging from the cafés half shaded by the trees that lined the square, carrying glasses of 'çay' which they distributed in exchange for a coin or two.

She and Mehmet sat at one of the cafés where they had a second breakfast of bread and yoghourt. The mayor had gone, but soon two men joined them and they all began chatting. The owner of the café kept bringing glasses of tea. They seemed to be exchanging jokes; their laughter reflected in the eyes of a man sitting two yards away on the doorstep of his shop between an oil jar and a bag of flour. Mehmet ate heartily, laughed with the men, but kept his gaze on the market. He didn't miss any of the exchanges that were taking place in front of him. After a last bite of bread, he stood up and entered the fray. For a while Marie followed him around the square as he checked the various kinds of wool on display. He knew most of the villagers and news and jokes were exchanged. But there was no question; this was no entertainment, it was serious business. What Mehmet was after was the best quality wool, patting it and pulling at as if it were alive. After a while, she lost track of him, her attention caught by a group of men who were arguing loudly; ready, it seemed, to come to blows but then ending up slapping each other on the back. A child, eyes wide with curiosity, suddenly stopped pulling at his mother's arm to look at the foreign woman. She smiled at the child who turned away and sank his face in his mother's skirt. As Marie took a few steps, she was arrested by the sight of a man who, his hand on his forehead, then his lips, then his heart, was bowing to an old man sitting beside a bundle of wool. She remembered noticing a similar scene at the otogar in Ankara while she waited for her coach to Konya. She found the gesture strangely moving and wished age would arouse the same respect in the West as here. At that moment, she felt a hand on her arm pushing her violently and, instinctively, she clasped her handbag to her side. She was about to protest when a horse pulling a cart passed a few inches away from her and stopped. She turned to thank the man who had kept her away from harm but he was already gone, lost in the crowd. She sighed; she was more disorientated than she thought. The man holding the reins was still on the cart when a younger one, perhaps his son, came up and, gestured towards the load in the cart, then to one of the sharp-eyed men sitting by the side. A tough bargaining ensued until a deal must have been struck, for trays of tea appeared and, soon afterwards, the cart and its driver moved by the side of the square where Marie watched the wool being loaded on to the back of a van.

Now where was Mehmet? She was trying to locate him when she noticed a man throwing baskets of chickens of various colours into a large cardboard box. The blue, pink, red and yellow chickens had clearly been dyed; this didn't mean though they were not destined for the pot. Almost immediately, a child, no more than eight years old, it seemed, approached and pointed at a bright yellow chicken which the man picked up by its legs and handed to him in exchange for a dirty creased bank note. A few seconds later the child was back, this time with his mother holding the yellow chicken. The merchant didn't argue and the chicken was promptly exchanged for a white one, apparently of better quality. How does one recognize a good chicken from a bad one? Marie wondered. She was thinking of the headless and featherless chickens in the supermarkets of the West, where 'progress' had squeezed life out of existence, when Mehmet appeared, a look of satisfaction on his face. 'I bought the wool,' he said. 'Good spring wool.' In Konya, he'd told her that the wool gathered in the spring had longer fibres than the one collected in summer, also that the very best wool came from young animals. 'It dyes better,' he'd said. She didn't doubt his words but how could he tell? All these bundles of grey, dirty wool looked the same to her.

The next step was to weigh the wool. Mehmet gestured towards two men each holding one end of a thick wooden stick that supported the scale: a simple metal bar marked with figures, with two copper cylinders – the weights – running along it. Each bundle of wool was hung from the bar and the weigh calculated by moving the cylinders along, a simple but reliable method. The operation took over twenty minutes, with Mehmet's gaze fixed all along on the bar – no one was going to cheat him. It was agreed that in total the weight amounted to a ton. Mehmet certainly didn't do things by half. He knew what he wanted and got it. Marie had noticed that even in the middle of this crowd, he stood out, exuding power and authority. She wondered how many carpets and kilims this ton of wool meant. And how was he to bring it to Konya? But there was more order than it seemed in the apparent chaos surrounding them. Mehmet was hardly gone when he came back accompanied by two men, the drivers of the lorry he had just hired, a blue and white truck parked at the corner of the square. Undeterred by the heat, Mehmet and the two drivers began loading the wool. In twenty minutes the job was done. Time to take to the road again or so Marie thought.

Mehmet had heard that in a village three miles away there was some good wool for sale, an opportunity he was not to miss. After a ten-minute drive, they came, followed by the lorry, to a dirt road that led to a hamlet of crumbling stone houses. Soon they were all sitting in the shade drinking glasses of *ayran*, the same drink of watered yoghourt Marie had already tasted in Istanbul. She looked around while the men talked. A few yards away, chickens were picking at the dry earth; a bunch of children were playing in the dust. One of them, a little boy, came up and stood looking at her, too shy to return her smile. The bargain was quickly struck and three more bags of wool joined the cargo on top of the lorry. At last, they were on their way.

The lorry would go first, Mehmet said. He and Marie would follow in the car. She couldn't help a sigh. By now the heat was at its worst and, with the lorry leading the way, it would take them at least an extra hour to get to Konya. Still, the whole experience had been worthwhile. Extraordinary to think that one day some of this wool would be a carpet in someone's sitting room at the other end of the world.

Marie stretched. She was still in bed and it was already eight. She had missed the call to prayer, her morning blessing as she called it. The previous day was still with her: the wool market and its hustle and bustle, the child with the yellow chicken, the guilty face of the lorry driver who, when they arrived in Konya, had damaged the garden wall of one of Mehmet's neighbours. It turned out that the driver had no licence. But this was Turkey. No one wanted the police and the law to interfere when everything could be settled amicably with a few bank notes. The memory made her smile. The angry neighbour had soon relaxed and, once unloaded, the wool had been dropped over Mehmet's courtyard, a stretch of cement running along his house. 'Tomorrow you come again,' he'd said after paying the two drivers. 'Tomorrow, we wash the wool. When it's clean, it loses half its weight.' As she wondered how the wool would dry, it all came back to her: the white flat roofs turning pink in the evening light as her coach entered the suburbs of Konya, the sight unreal, magical. How could those brick houses be covered in white? They were in the middle of July, it couldn't be snow. She must have looked puzzled. 'Wool,' said the woman sitting next to her. 'Wool,' she repeated. Marie nodded, wondering why these people kept wool on their roofs in the middle of summer. Now it all made sense. The wool was drying under the scorching Turkish sun.

She shook herself and jumped out of bed. This was no time to stay in bed. Down in the restaurant, she gulped the usual breakfast of tea and bread and yoghourt accompanied with slices of tomatoes and cucumber. At the shop, Mehmet was ready. 'Today we wash the wool,' he said by way of welcome. He left his father in charge and they got to the car parked in front of the shop.

'You take photos, yes?' Mehmet said as they gathered speed. She was glad he suggested it. She had taken plenty of photographs in the wool market, but she'd thought his family might not like it. The car suddenly jerked. A van emerging from a side road had missed them by a few inches. 'Mad man!' Mehmet was shaking his head. 'These people don't know how to drive.' But his mind was already on something else. 'You'll have lunch with us; my mother is good cook. She'll show you the garden. We have all the vegetables: carrots, potatoes, onions, we always have plenty to eat.' His pride was touching, like that of a child who has just taken his first steps, and, Marie suspected, a child who had known hunger. 'Who takes care of the garden?' she asked. 'Your mother?' 'Yes, my mother and my sisters. I have three sisters. One is married; her husband also helps.' Marie was beginning to build a picture. This man was not only driven by ambition, he carried his whole family with him.

'Lots of women in my house,' Mehmet said as he opened the metal gate to the courtyard. On the right, a flight of stairs led to the inhabited part of the house. 'Today my sisters, they come and they bring their friends to help.' He didn't mention his wife. 'She is a modern woman,' he'd once told her, 'she has a job; she is a nurse.'

Two of his younger sisters lived in the house with his mother and also the 'modern' wife and their two daughters, Bilge, seven and Dida, only two. He must be glad to have a brother, Marie thought. All these women; it must be overwhelming at times. The mother and the wife were waiting on top of the stairs with the young daughters, two worlds standing next to each other: Mehmet's mother, head covered, traditional baggy trousers, and beside her, the wife, head uncovered, skirt ending just below the knees with, on top, a simple blue sweater; the daughters both wearing short summer dresses.

Marie was ushered into a large sitting room with a balcony. 'You go and look,' Mehmet said to Marie before they sat and drank the tea one of his sisters was bringing in. The balcony looked over the courtyard where half a dozen women with head scarves, their trousers tucked in rubber boots, were stamping on the wool scattered around. Another woman, armed with a hose, was spraying the wool with water. As Marie looked, she saw Mehmet joining them and taking hold of the hose. Floods of dirty water were running in the gutters on each side of the yard: a colourful scene which Marie was glad to photograph. One of the women looked up and waved to her. She felt embarrassed at being caught watching while everybody else was working. But perhaps a book could emerge from her photographs.

By lunchtime, they were all sitting together on the floor of the sitting room sharing fresh salad and homemade yoghourt. The woman sitting next to Marie, one of Mehmet's sisters, asked her in broken English whether she knew of a cream that could heal the chilblain on her hands. Marie didn't know of any, and Mehmet, who had heard, shrugged away his sister's request. 'It's nothing,' he said. 'She doesn't need cream.' Life was tough and women's hands were for working. No need to complain. Mehmet might be proud of his modern wife, but in his world, there was little room for the needs and complaints of women. They ate eagerly then went back to the washing. It was late afternoon when the dripping wool was finally spread on the low walls that surrounded the yard, as well as on the long wooden beams that Mehmet had set up on top of trestles.

Mehmet was to drive Marie back to her hotel, but before that, he wanted her to look at the garden. He exchanged a few words with his mother who nodded and, with a serious face, took Marie to the large plot of land on the other side of the house where they grew their food. Together, they walked through neat rows of carrots, leeks, spinach, lettuce and even corn. From time to time, the woman leaned to pick an onion or tear off a withered leaf. There was enough here to feed a large family. In a corner, a plum tree spread its branches heavy with purple fruit. They walked slowly, Mehmet's mother making sure that Marie didn't miss anything. Though they didn't share a language, there was no need for words. The woman's face reflected a mixture of pride and quiet contentment. This was her domain, the place where she and her daughters spent hours planting, watering and picking the food that sustained the family. But she was not only proud of her garden, Marie sensed. Her son had built a business out of nothing; he had brought his parents and sisters from their village to Konya; he had built the house where they lived and grew their food. Thanks to him, their life had expanded; this woman, his mother, was perhaps a little in awe of him; yet, in one way or another, everyone in the family had taken part in this upward move. Life was good and she was grateful. A moment later, as Marie and Mehmet prepared to leave, the two women hugged each other.

Though nothing much was happening, time was flying. Every morning, Marie crossed the road to pay her visit to the shrine where the guard on duty now gave her a nod of recognition when she entered. The place was like a magnet, and sometimes in the late afternoon she felt an urge to make another visit. She expected, or rather hoped, that the same overwhelming feeling of love that had flooded her the previous month would come again but she felt nothing. Empty of feelings, she stood there watching the incessant flow of bewildered tourists, the pilgrims silently praying, and yet she still felt unable to leave and stayed longer than she had planned.

Only three days left before going back to Istanbul and then home. Marie didn't want to think about it. Mehmet had promised to take her and his family this Sunday to his village in the Taurus Mountains, the day before she was to leave. They would have a picnic on the way, he'd said.

In the meantime, Marie would take a few more photographs in order to have a complete picture of the process of carpet making. She'd been told of a village nearby where the women spun the wool. This was done in the traditional way, on drop spindles. The spinning season had not yet started, it was too early, but the women wouldn't mind showing her.

The village, five miles away, was called Sille. She took a taxi and by six o'clock – the heat had begun to recede – they were parking beside a fountain next to a group of stone houses crumbling under the sun. Half hidden behind a curtain of poplars, Marie glimpsed a dry riverbed, although the fountain brimmed with water, suggesting the presence of underground pipes. A woman offered them two glasses of water. Marie asked the driver to explain that she would like to see how the wool was spun, even though she knew this was not the right time of year. The woman nodded and with her hand indicated that Marie was to follow her. It was the same as with Mehmet's family: no pretence, no sign of servility, just simple kindness and hospitality. In the entrance a loom, with half a carpet already woven, left barely any space to walk. The woman took Marie to the back of the house and to a courtyard where another loom was set up under the shade of a tree. Near the loom, an older woman, busy peeling potatoes, looked up, smiled then went back to her task. A bunch of giggling children was playing around. A little girl with green eyes ran out of the group, and with a wide smile sat at the loom, eager to show off her skill. She couldn't have been more than nine. Her fingers seemed to move by themselves as they pulled and wove the thread of different colours through the weft. A small faded photograph fixed on top of the loom showed the pattern she was to follow. She didn't seem to look at it, yet there were no flaws in her weaving. The first woman smiled, shaking her head at the child. She went inside then came back with a ball of carded wool and a curious wooden tool – a cross fixed around a longer piece of wood. Standing with the wool in her left hand, she pulled at it with her other hand and thinned it into a fine and regular thread. The thread of wool was attached to the spinning tool and as the woman kept thinning the wool, it began turning on itself to form a small ball around the wooden cross. The woman's movements were quick and steady; it looked easy but Marie was not surprised when, offered to try, she found that the wool came either too thick or too thin through her fingers until it finally broke. They all laughed. She would have to practise a lot more before she could spin a proper ball of wool. She left the village, touched once again by the kindness of the people.

In a few weeks – she would be gone. The dry wool would be brought to the villages and the women would begin to spin. After that, the yarns would go back to the owner of the wool to be dyed. And then balls of wool of various colours would be distributed to the families with a small photograph of the pattern to weave. During the long winter months, the women would sit at their looms with sometimes a child at their side learning the craft. For a moment, Marie envied them. These people seemed to possess what she was yearning for: a sense of meaning, a sense of belonging. Never again would she look at a carpet without thinking of them.

That evening in her room, Marie jotted down her memories of the day: the woman spinning the wool, the young girl with green eyes, the loom with its half-woven carpet, and then the grandmother with the children all pausing with serious faces for her to take their photograph. Observing these people and being admitted in their life was a privilege; it was also a distraction. She had not thought much about Alex these last few days but she'd also lost the contact with Rumi and with God. She still went to the Museum but it had become a sort of ritual which had left her heart unmoved. And if her heart was not alive, what was the point of it all? She fell asleep feeling once again that her life lacked purpose, that she was caught in a meaningless web from which she would never escape. Please help, she cried silently, not sure to whom she was addressing her prayer, but perhaps this didn't matter. Asking was perhaps enough.

Paris 2014

Now she wonders. Why this obsession with the making of carpets? She had never seriously thought of a book on the subject; she didn't have the expertise or the necessary determination. To forget Alex? That may have been the obvious reason, but twenty years later her research in carpet making looks curiously symbolic, as if, at the time, an invisible hand was guiding her and making tangible the harmony hidden at the core of life.

Konya – July 1997

She spent the next day walking through the bazaar in search of gifts to take back to England. The old man sitting on the steps of his tiny shop asked her as she peered through the door if she was German. As she said that no, she was French, he told her he had worked for two years in France in a town called Epinal. Had she been there? No, she knew of it, but had never been there. Now standing up, the man went inside and came back with two pairs of hand knitted socks made of rough white wool. Their shape was unusual, the heels as well as the front of the foot were pointed and a motif ran along both sides of the leg. This was such beautiful craftsmanship that she couldn't resist buying them both. She was going to leave, when he made a sign for her to wait then disappeared in the back of the shop. He returned with a piece of silk, which he spread in front of her. Actually, it was a large maroon shawl embroidered all along with white, orange and red motifs, similar to those she had seen on some of the carpets. This was unusual; she had not been shown anything like this in any of the shops she had explored. 'This, traditional Uzbek,' the man said as he handed her the shawl. The whole piece was made of very fine silk with the motifs embroidered on top of the weaving; it carried the flavour of a world that knew nothing of time, and where beauty was born out of careful patient hands. It must have taken months, perhaps a year, to make it, or perhaps it was a team work when mothers, sisters and daughters had worked at it together. Was the man grateful for her appreciation? She wondered. The quiet sparkle in his eyes lit his wrinkled face. She was going to ask him how much he wanted for the shawl when, before she'd said a word, he quoted a ridiculously low price. This would be worth a fortune in London, she thought. She didn't hesitate and nodded. There it was. The shawl was hers. He folded it in a thin piece of paper and handed it to her. As she went, she wondered whether this was not a gift. She turned back; the man was sitting once again in front of his shop, looking straight in front of him, his face expressionless.

On her way to the Dergah, she stopped to look at a stand of postcards. Until now, she had ignored them but she was close to leaving and, once back in England, she would regret not to have bought a few. There were several views of the Green Dome above Rumi's resting place, as well as photographs of the ceramics exhibited in the Karatay museum, which she had visited at the beginning of her stay: exquisite tiles showing a gazelle jumping in the air, fish around the face of a woman, a rabbit, all of them in tones of blue and green, all dating back to the Seljuks, the time of Rumi. The huge round stone, part of the dome of a mosque and decorated with an intricate design over a turquoise background, was also among the cards. She picked five of them and handed a note to the young man standing at the door, who, instead of taking the note, invited her inside. Well, she could always have a glass of tea as no doubt he would offer her. 'I am not buying anything else,' she warned him. 'No problem,' he said, shaking his head. 'You no need to buy something.' The place was not very big – about half the size of Mehmet's shop – and apart from the expected piles of kilims and carpets in a corner, there were the usual trinkets for tourists. Against a wall, a large glass cabinet took most of the space; it contained some silver jewellery with, on top, rows of whirling dervishes of different sizes and colours. Thin, dark-haired, the shopkeeper was not very different from all the young men in Konya or Istanbul. They all seemed to wear the same pair of jeans and white T-shirt, and all were keen to draw the prospective client into their shop or to someone else's shop where a sale would earn them a commission. He offered her a chair and sat down on the edge of an old sofa next to a small table. He looked shy, almost embarrassed. He gave her a quick look then asked, 'Would you like tea?'

'Yes, that would be nice.' He jumped up and disappeared in the back of the shop. A moment later, he was back with two glasses of tea. As he handed her hers, he stuttered, 'I need to speak good English. You, help me?' So this was what he was after.

'Yes, of course,' she said, 'but not for too long.' He smiled, apparently relieved, and picked the worn-out book that lay on the table. 'This, English book,' he said, handing her the dog-eared volume, a novel by an unknown author, its cover long gone. 'This too difficult,' he said. The little he knew, he must have learnt from passing tourists. 'I need to learn more,' he said. There was a hint of desperation in his voice. She thought of Mehmet, and how little these men possessed to start and build a life for themselves. She was not in a hurry and he looked so eager. If she could help him even a little, why not? She stayed almost an hour, correcting his most obvious mistakes. 'No, you don't say "his scarf" when it belongs to a woman, you say, "her scarf".' His pronunciation was not bad; learning through listening has its advantages. She paid for her postcards and wished him good luck before crossing the road to her hotel.

They started early. Mehmet's car was in front of the hotel at seven-thirty, as promised. First, he said, they were to go and fetch a couple and their boy. Marie wondered where his wife and their two daughters were, but said nothing. They picked up the couple and the boy. 'Now we go and fetch Seva, my wife,' Mehmet said. She was standing on the steps of the house when they arrived, and a few minutes later, Mehmet's mother waved at them from the door when they left with Seva and the two girls. Marie was sitting in the front, between the two men, while in the back, Seva and the other woman sat each with a child on her lap. The children were shushed; they were at last on their way. Well, not before a stop at the butcher, and then at the cooperative to deliver the bags of pears packed in the boot of the car. It was ten past nine, and by now the coolness of the morning had gone. They were finally leaving Konya, the car now taking speed on the long ribbon of asphalt that split the plain in two. The engine purred, the two women chatted and Mehmet whistled. 'You'll see my village; I'll take you,' he had said several times, his face beaming with anticipation. 'It's beautiful there in the mountains.' Yes, he missed his village, he said, 'but life is too hard for the people there; they have no money. I try help them.' They stopped to get water at a spring then once more in a small town to buy milk and to drop the couple and their boy.

The landscape began to change; the dry open space of the plain with its rare flocks of sheep giving way to small hills hollowed out by erosion and covered in shrubs. At some point, they left the main road and took a winding strip with, on both sides, mixed vegetation of pines and bushes. It was around noon when Mehmet parked the car along a group of thorny bushes near a stream and announced, 'We stop for picnic now.' They spread a kilim on the ground then unpacked while Mehmet assembled a rudimentary stove which he filled with charcoal. The stove was made of aluminium, on top of which he fitted a small chimney. Half an hour later, a smell of frying chicken filled the air. They ate with relish, tearing at the bread and picking shredded pieces of lettuce and the inevitable slices of cucumber and tomatoes from a plastic box.

They were finishing their meal when Mehmet pulled out a bottle of whisky which he offered to Marie who refused, and from which he then ostentatiously drank large mouthfuls, no doubt for her benefit, his way of proclaiming his disdain for the clerics and their religious rules. She made no comment and he soon fell asleep.

Not a sound except for the buzzing of insects and Mehmet's intermittent snoring. Would they ever reach the village? The heat was stifling, the air a suffocating cloak that clung to the skin. With the back of her hand Marie wiped her forehead, wet with perspiration. Was boredom only a Western disease? It didn't seem to affect the people here. Was it because they had a different sense of time from hers? Theirs was apparently unconstrained with no clear beginning or end. It just flowed. The two year old was asleep on Seva's lap, her sister playing with pebbles and sticks near the stream. Their mother seemed perfectly content. Marie wished they could talk together but apart from a few English words, the two women had no language in common. As for lying down, the rough terrain was hardly inviting. She must have dozed though as she started when Mehmet announced that it was time to move.

The road had become steep and twisting as they gained altitude. 'My village is almost two thousand metres high,' Mehmet had told her. The earth, ochre until then, had turned red; the oaks and birches had given place to firs, and on the horizon, the gigantic arena of the mountain ranges expanded in various shades of purple. There was something majestic about this landscape and yet it didn't crush you; it made you larger, part of it. The car took a last curve and there it was: a group of stone houses huddled together on the hill facing them, washed in gold in the evening light – Mehmet's village. They approached slowly and stopped beside the fountain near the first houses, people surging from everywhere. Mehmet, the successful son, was paying them a visit. The children pushed, shoved and sparred with each other to get closer; the women cheered and clapped their hands, faces beaming, the whole village in a mood of celebration.

A woman approached, took Marie's hand in hers then kissed Seva, the two girls and finally Mehmet himself on both cheeks. She was not very different from his own mother: the same tired face tanned by the sun, the same expression of quiet contentment that said that life was hard but worth living. But most striking were her eyes as well as those of everyone around. Marie had never seen so much light in people's eyes. It was as if they had been washed in the mountain springs; they shone.

The village was almost at the same level as the mountains that rose around them on the horizon. They seemed to be standing on top of the world, right in the centre of this landscape that reflected in their eyes. Here, as though waiting for her, was what she had been unable to find at the mausoleum, that power that consoles, nourishes and cures all pains and which, Rumi says, is always at hand. His words jumped to her mind: *'Keep silent; bathe in this wonder.'* She turned away to hide her tears.

Mehmet was gazing beyond the houses with an appreciative

look at the slopes covered in vines. 'The grapes soon ready for Konya,' he said. But his mind was on something else. 'You come and see.' He was pointing at a small ladder posted against one of the houses, and was already climbing, Bilge just behind him. Marie followed them. Just a few steps upward and there, spread over the roof terraces, were rows and rows of coloured kilims. 'With the sun,' Mehmet had once told her, 'the colours change, they become stronger, particularly the reds.' The display was unexpected, though curiously the colours, far from jarring with the surroundings, gave a dreaming quality to the whole scenery. If someone had told her that one of these kilims was the renowned magic carpet of the *One Thousand and One Nights*, she would have believed it. 'Whoever sits on this carpet will, in the twinkling of an eye, be borne thither to that place near hand or distant many a day's journey.' The archaic phrasing her grand-mother had read to her had jumped back. If the magic carpet were there, would it take her to Alex? Would it erase the past? The thought had annoyingly intruded. She closed her eyes to dismiss it. Words came up, neither voiced nor written, though vivid, 'Don't miss the present.' When she opened her eyes again, there was Mehmet, his back to her, inspecting his kilims, Bilge jumping from one kilim to another in a game of her own, and all around, the arena of mountain ranges. This was the real magic. She tried to count the kilims but they were too many. Fifty, perhaps more; she lost count. Mehmet turned to her, his face full of proud satisfaction. 'They stay here another month then I bring them back to Konya.' The way he talked of his kilims, they could have been living creatures.

They rejoined the others on the roof where they had first been greeted. In one corner, two more kilims were soaking up the sun, giving the scene an improbable air of luxury. Mehmet and Marie sat down. A young girl brought a pot of tea and began filling glasses, which she passed around. A younger girl came up and, as if it were the most natural thing in the world, went round and kissed everyone including Marie twice on the cheeks. Seva offered the biscuits she had brought while Mehmet talked with the man of the house and Marie exchanged smiles with the woman. It was that time of day when nature recovers its breath. Dida, the two year old, had fallen asleep, her head resting on her mother's lap, Bilge was quietly turning the pages of a children's book; the men kept chatting. In front of them, the silhouette of the minaret stood out against a sky ablaze. How was it, Marie wondered, that she had not heard the muezzin? The mosque was only a few yards away. Why was the call to prayer so discreet here? Was it at the request of the villagers? Marie thought that here God was so close that these people had little need for intermediaries. Their lives were rich, not in the way of the West, for they had few possessions. Doctors and dentists were a luxury they could not afford, electricity had come late and most of the young men were in Istanbul earning money, yet the shine in their eyes didn't lie. Did they know that they were happier than many of the people in the cities? Or was she romanticising? Life in these villages was harsh, winters meant mud, ice and snow, and lasted months. Still, there was a peace here she had rarely encountered anywhere else. She let herself drift away, savouring the coolness of the air, feeling vaguely that, whatever her moves, everything was exactly as it was supposed to be and that trying to foresee the future was a waste of energy.

They left with the last rays of sun disappearing behind the mountains. A thin silvery crescent was slowly rising on the dark blue of the coming night. This had been an incredible gift of a day.

On the way back, they stopped for a last picnic. The mountain air had made them hungry; they spread the old kilim and quickly finished the leftover of their lunch. Later on in her room, Marie marked the day in her diary as 'the day Rumi made himself known again.'

She returned to London filled with the colours and images of Turkey, the faces of the people, the immensity of the landscapes. She resumed her weekly visits to Jean and together they laughed at the world and its absurdities. The book of quotations was selling well and life was becoming bearable without Alex. One day, as Jean was applying pressure on her shoulder, asking her how it felt, Marie on an impulse put her arms around her. 'This place is magic,' she said, 'and you are the fairy.' Jean, Marie knew, was not prone to demonstrative affection; she also refused any suggestion that she was a teacher or guru. She pondered Marie's remark then, 'I can accept that,' she said, trying not to smile.

A year went. Kayan's meetings were still taking place. But as time went on, Marie found it more and more difficult to attend. The Arabic invocations were too foreign; this made her feel like a traitor to the group. Kayan was gently pushing them into practising the Muslim prayer, something she found impossible. Praying in Arabic didn't make sense. She watched the others fall on their knees in ritual prostration but she abstained. Yes, Rumi was a Muslim, and in his time, many around him and through him had converted. 'But this is not my culture,' Marie kept saying. Torn between her loyalty to Kayan and loyalty to herself, she felt confused. Was she following the right path? Couldn't she apply Rumi's teaching to her life and not be a Muslim?

There was no use brooding; she turned to the quotations and, as her friend Robbie had suggested, began writing. She covered the various stages of Rumi's life, his childhood, his becoming a renowned religious teacher, then the encounter with Shams the mysterious dervish who was to change his life, and finally, the agonising grief at Shams' disappearance. Intertwined in the story were quotations picked out of her book. After a few months, the result was not quite a play. 'A staged meditation,' Robbie suggested. A good idea, she thought, but whatever it was – play or meditation – she couldn't continue alone. She had no experience of the theatre, and if this was to be staged, she needed actors as well as a director. She contacted Sue, her friend of forty years. She would be the ideal person to direct the play and she might like the challenge. She and her husband had travelled the world teaching Shakespeare under the auspices of the British Arts Council; Sue had done some work at Covent Garden. 'The play,' Marie told her, 'is based on the life of Rumi and on his teaching, not quite your field.' Would she be interested? Yes, she was interested. True, she knew little about Rumi but his spiritual teaching attracted her. Marie still had to find the actors. Once again, destiny! One afternoon, after a session with Jean, she caught sight of a poster in a pub window. There, was the well-known picture of a pensive Rumi, his hands hidden in the folds of his cloak. Ashley R... a storyteller, said the poster, would be reciting stories and poems of Rumi the next evening. It seemed like a sign. Marie didn't hesitate. The pub was no more than five minutes' walk from her studio. It might, of course, be one of those performances when bits and pieces of Rumi's poems are offered pell-mell, beautifully recited but without any context or connection between the pieces.

The following evening, among an audience of some forty people, Marie was sitting in the back room of the pub. The place was full. The storyteller was of medium-build with curly chestnut hair and a face that expressed a mixture of fragility and forcefulness. He must have been in his forties and transmitted the intensity of Rumi with a sobriety that was more effective than Alex's passionate excesses. There was still no context, but at least, without falling into the trap of sentimentality, the man had arranged the poems in a way that moved the heart. She was not disappointed.

After the performance, Marie went to congratulate the performer and tell him about her project. Could he contemplate taking part in something like a play about Rumi's life and teaching? 'Tell me more,' he said, already interested. 'The purpose,' said Marie, 'is to show how Rumi came to write what he wrote and, through quotations, to expose the various aspects of his teaching. In a sense,' she added, 'the play – I don't know what to call it – is about the impact of the encounter with Shams.' Ashley was listening attentively. She explained that she had in mind two actors, one who would be Rumi, the other Shams. Leaning against the wall, Ashley nodded. Yes, he liked the idea. She asked, did he know someone else who could act with him? Actually he did. 'I have a friend, he's also a storyteller and recites poems by Rumi, and he might well be interested,' he said. The friend's name was Duncan. Ashley would talk to him. They exchanged phone numbers and she left feeling that a big step had been taken.

February 1998

Several weeks later, Sue along with the two storytellers met at Marie's place for a first reading. Duncan was very different from Ashley: taller, dark straight hair with sharp features that could have been carved with a knife. He looked like a quiet volcano whose well-contained power could erupt at any moment.

Sue did the reading and it became clear that the script needed improvement. Though her heart sank at the thought of making changes – there was so much of her in this piece – Marie had to admit that the play was too abrupt, that it needed to expand. The question was not about who owned the play; what mattered was for it to work. Ashley suggested adding other translations of Rumi's work as well as some extra details about his life. Sue remarked that this was not like radio, or a book, where things need to be described. 'The action on stage tells it all,' she said. But as long as the framework remained and the quotations she had chosen were retained, Marie could accept, even welcome the changes. Choosing a title was easier; they all agreed on *Love's Journey*. Things were beginning to take shape. They also agreed that the play would be performed on three consecutive nights at the end of May. That gave them three months.

In the meantime, Marie would take care of the publicity and look for a venue. There was also the question of music necessary to generate the atmosphere of devotion and sacredness the play required. Marie was clear; no other music than the traditional music of the Mevlevi would do, which meant finding a *ney* player as well as a drummer. She thought of Robin. He belonged to her Sufi group and had learnt to play the *ney* in Turkey. But he wouldn't be easy to persuade. He was known for refusing to perform in public. Would he make an exception for her? On the phone, he was far from enthusiastic. When they met, as expected, he first said no. Only once he was convinced that the play was really an act of devotion and not a commercial enterprise did he accept. He also knew a drummer who, he said, would certainly say yes. This is not a concert, Marie warned him. What she had in mind was a short opening piece before the actors appeared then brief moments, no more than a minute or two at most to underline a mood or create a breathing space at the most intense moments. Robin nodded while admitting this was not something he was used to. 'I play following my feelings,' he said, 'and sometimes for as long as ten minutes at a time.'

'It will be all right,' she reassured him. 'We'll be working as a team.' She immediately knew this was a mistake. Robin was a lone wolf. Teamwork was not something he would welcome. But he didn't go back on his decision.

A week later, Ashley produced a more fleshy script. He had enlarged the narrative and added quite a few more poems. Relieved, Marie had to admit that the new version had lost none of its intensity and was, in fact, more potent.

After some research, Marie chose the Kufa Gallery as the venue. Located on Westbourne Grove, it had the advantage of being easily accessible by bus or by tube. Run by Iraqi refugees, the place consisted of two large rooms that were often used for art exhibitions. The main room, she was told, could contain as many as eighty people. The anteroom, she thought, would be perfect to check in the entries and allow people to chat before and after the show. There was no problem renting the place for three nights at the end of May. She now could have the programmes printed.

End of March/April 1998

The rehearsals had just started when Marie received a letter from her doctor saying that, after her recent check-up, further examination, this time under anaesthetic, was necessary. Would she contact him to fix a date? It would take place at the Hammersmith Hospital; she would not need to be hospitalized for more than half a day. Boring stuff, Marie thought. She had more important things to do and she didn't want to miss any of the rehearsals that had just started. Only the day before, she had attended the first one in the old school in Sussex where Ashley taught storytelling.

Though her presence was not needed – Sue was in charge – Marie had found the experience exhilarating. It was extraordinary to see her words, as well as Rumi's, coming to life. Sue had decided that the two actors would alternatively be three different persons: Rumi and Shams and also the narrator, and it worked. Far from being confusing, the alternation, through the use of movements, enhanced the enfolding of the drama, bringing it to life.

Sue was brilliant at triggering the men's different temperaments: Ashley self-contained and at times too reserved, Duncan whose passion needed harnessing but was contagious. She teased and laughed but remained firm, drawing from them both the reaction or the move she wanted.

She and Robbie were sitting in one of the Hammersmith Hospital waiting rooms, as dull and sterile as one could expect. 'Please, Dr Anderson will now see you.' Marie looked at the nurse standing in front of her, a tall fierce-looking woman who, Marie couldn't help noticing, looked slightly embarrassed; she wondered why. The nurse motioned her into a small room where a doctor in a white coat was sitting behind a table. He stood up and offered her the chair in front of it. 'Please sit down,' he said. 'You have a friend with you?' She nodded. 'Would you like her to come in and sit with you?' The offer felt incongruent. Why should she impose her exchange with a doctor on her friend, and anyway, it was a little too personal.

'No, I prefer not.' He didn't insist and went straight to the point.

'Well, this is not very good news, I'm afraid.' He paused for a second and, 'It is cancer and it is aggressive.' For some reason, it was the word aggressive that had caught her attention.

'It's like me,' she said, laughing. The doctor didn't laugh; he didn't even smile.

'We need to operate soon,' he continued. 'And,' he sounded apologetic, 'afterwards you will need radiotherapy as well as chemotherapy.' She was hardly listening. No, she thought, this is not the time; there were only six weeks to go before the first performance.

'Can't it wait?' she asked. He shifted on his chair. She couldn't tell if her question embarrassed or surprised him.

'It depends what you mean by wait,' he said.

'Six months?' she asked.

'No,' he shook his head, 'not six months; one or two at most.' She sighed. All she could think of was the play, the rehearsals she wanted to attend, the programmes that still needed printing, the *ney* player and his unpredictable changes of moods.

That evening she had dinner at Robbie's from where she phoned her sister to let her know. 'Don't tell Mum,' she said. She couldn't afford to spill her energy in dealing with their mother's worries. At the same time, she felt very calm, as if someone else had been diagnosed. I should be frightened, she thought, but all she felt was a sense of estrangement. The threat was not so much the disease itself, but the word, cancer. Turning back on the doorstep as she left Robbie, 'I am still me,' she said, somehow surprised at her remark. She had just discovered that having cancer didn't mean one belonged to a different species.

She didn't sleep well that night. It was as if an alarm bell kept ringing somewhere in the background, warning her that, whatever she thought, the sword of Damocles was hanging over her head and that pretending it was not there was not going to work. Going day after day with the knowledge that within her body an enemy was gnawing at her, life would be impossible. As well as the cancer, anxiety would make her ill.

It was just after nine in the morning when she phoned the hospital. 'Can I speak to Dr Anderson?'

'I don't know where…' the nurse began then, 'you're lucky, I just see him coming up the corridor, I'll pass him to you.'

'I'm so relieved you called,' he said when he recognized her voice. She explained that she had decided after all to have the operation as soon as possible. He didn't waste time. 'My secretary will arrange an appointment for you this morning,' he said. 'Ring back in half an hour; she'll let you know the exact time.' An hour later Marie was driving to the Hammersmith Hospital where she was to report to Mr McIndoe's clinic at eleven-thirty. She might have to wait, the secretary warned, but Marie would definitely be seen that morning.

The waiting room was full. She had been squeezed between the regular patients, and she prepared to wait. She looked around. Were they all cancer patients? A thin young woman was leafing absently through a magazine; the old Asian man sitting crossed arms beside her repressed a yawn. It all seemed so normal. None of these faces seemed particularly worried: the man with a neat grey beard reading his paper, the child whining on her mother's lap, the nurse calling names from time to time; a sample of humanity that could have been found in any waiting room, in a train station or a beauty parlour. But of course, no one wants to go around with a label attached around his/her neck saying, 'Beware, I am mortally ill.' Was this a special kind of waiting room, the waiting room to eternity? Would St Peter appear at the corner? This was a silly thought. These people were not waiting for eternity; they were waiting to be told that they would steer free from their illness; that they would soon be back in their interrupted lives.

It was close to one o'clock when she came face to face with the surgeon, a man in his early fifties who said that her operation could be planned for this coming Tuesday. No operation could take place the day before as it was Easter Monday, a bank holiday. 'Unfortunately,' he said, 'I'm away the whole coming week.' She had the choice between waiting for his return or having the operation immediately. 'I have total confidence in my team,' he added, 'but it is up to you to decide.' She hesitated.

'Can I ring you in about an hour?' she asked, unable to make up her mind on the spot.

'Yes, of course, here is my secretary's number. But whatever you decide, I can assure you it won't make any difference in terms of the operation itself.' By the time she was home, she was clear. As she'd just experienced, action was empowering. Waiting only even a week wouldn't do her any good; she would only be brooding. The long weekend was going to be difficult enough. At least, no time was being wasted. She was to register at the hospital on Monday; the operation would take place the next morning.

Easter Monday – April 1998

She found the hospital dozing in the early afternoon, almost empty of staff. The room she was in was on the first floor and contained at least a dozen beds, all enclosed behind curtains. She thought of the French hospitals with their so-called private room, which the patient shares with another patient: no curtain separating the beds so that the two of them have also to share each other's visitors as well as the one television set provided without individual earphones, a nightmare.

The blue-uniformed nurse on duty, a woman in her forties, showed her a bed close to the nurses' office and handed her a hospital nightdress. 'You can place your clothes inside the bedside table,' she indicated. Marie sat on the bed surrounded by the curtain that defined her space. In the distance, the muffled roar of the traffic belonged to that other world of the rehearsal, of the *ney* player and his moods, of the programmes someone would have to take to the printer; it had all receded in the background. They were now in charge. Her priority was to face what was coming her way: the operation, this new curtained space, the smile of a nurse and, of course, the treatments once the operation was over. She had changed gears. After first going through neutral and only feeling numb, she had entered a new mode. It had all happened in the space of twenty-four hours; one day she was making plans for the weeks and the months to come, and then the future had stopped. It had not disappeared; but right now, there was only the present moment. She was on a new adventure, and it was exciting.

She undressed, folded her clothes and, with some relief, let herself slip into the softness of the bed. It had been a busy and tense morning. She could now relax. The privacy of the curtain was comforting while the presence of other patients felt faintly reassuring. As if to confirm her thought, a woman a few yards away cleared her throat. I should be afraid, she told herself. Odjar, one of the women in Kayan's group, had used the word victim saying that it was not fair to be ill. But Marie didn't feel like this at all. So many people had cancer, why not her? And anyway, this time tomorrow, the tumour would be gone. She closed her eyes; the real danger was not the cancer but the negative thoughts. A few days earlier, she had laughed when Robbie had told her that their friend Martin had complained that

Marie didn't leave any room for commiseration. Of course! She wasn't going to let anyone, including herself, put her in the category of victim or 'poor me'. This was not a wilful decision; it was pure instinct. Even the word surviving was dangerous; it opened the gates to all sorts of poisonous thoughts. What she needed was to keep her mind empty of anything connected to her illness. 'You are a fighter, so fight,' the nurse had said last week after the doctor had told her she had cancer. So unexpected had been the nurse's words that she had found nothing to say. How did she know Marie was a fighter? And was she? But she did sense that keeping her energy was absolutely essential, that the least pessimistic thought had to be quickly pushed away, and that anyone expressing doubt, fear or dread around her should be avoided and, as with her mother, kept in ignorance.

She must have dozed for she started when a nurse pulled the curtain. 'This is meal time,' she said, 'but tonight, I'm sorry; you're not allowed any food until after your operation.' She was a young girl, with a face more used to scrubbing than make-up; the wisp of blond hair that escaped from her cap still accentuating her childlike appearance. 'But you can have a drink of water,' she added with a smile. 'Would you like one?' Marie acquiesced. She knew the rules regulating an operation. 'I'll bring you a sleeping pill later on,' the nurse said. She pulled the curtain behind her and was gone. Thank God for the sleeping pill, Marie thought. She didn't want to spend the night worrying.

It was nine o'clock when she was wheeled towards the operating theatre. The anaesthetist took hold of her arm and unloaded the syringe into her vein. That was her last memory, then everything was gone.

Reconstruction

The first thing she saw when she opened her eyes was Robbie's tensed face. She tried to say hello but her jaw was tight and her mouth seemed to be filled with cotton wool. 'I can't speak,' she managed to mumble. A smile of relief had appeared on her friend's face.

'Don't try to speak. You frightened me. You were grey when I arrived.' Robbie paused, obviously reassured. 'The nurse told me the operation went well,' she said. Marie felt all right, a little groggy perhaps but that was to be expected. Only that lingering question in the back of her mind: had the cancer spread?

The next morning, the surgeon accompanied by a group of students came to check on her, and Marie immediately asked her question. Turning halfway towards her, halfway towards his students, 'We don't know yet,' he said, quickly adding, 'I'm sorry, we won't know before Friday. We have to wait for the results of the biopsies.' She was left to digest the news. She had three days of uncertainty in front of her. The surgeon and his students had already moved to the next patient.

During the following days, every time she thought that the cancer might have spread, she dived into her book. It was a travel book about modern China, interesting enough to keep her attention focused, but not too exciting to tire her or keep her awake at night. It became a sort of game. She could feel the thought almost tangible coming towards her, but as soon as it was too close, she mentally said, 'No, I don't want you,' and went back to the page she had been reading a second before. Sometimes, when she reached the end of a chapter and paused in her reading, it was not a thought that came but just a vague feeling of apprehension which, she knew, could easily turn into fear if she let it take root. Then she closed her eyes and summoned the letters N O in her mind's eyes, and only then returned to her reading. Curiously, it worked. The feeling or the thought drifted away, and when it didn't do so immediately, she whispered to herself that she meant it, that she wanted peace, no insinuations of any sort. This was the kind of mental gymnastics she had been practising for years, since RezaLeah had introduced her to meditation. She was not even sure she knew how to meditate or what meditation actually was. But with time, her mind had acquired a sort of elasticity that now proved useful. She remembered the days, before RezaLeah, when fear, guilt or shame took over and how she used to go on shopping sprees that only gave her temporary relief. It seemed that, little by little, without her being aware of it, she had learnt to live at peace with herself. And right now, peace was the foundation of her strength.

She recovered quickly from the operation. At the hospital, the woman doctor in charge of the follow-up treatments told her there was no time to waste. There was, she said, a forty-five per cent chance that the cancer could recur. Marie was to start chemotherapy the next day, a total of six sessions with an interval of three weeks in between to allow her blood to recuperate, after which there would be six weeks of radiotherapy – five times a week. Well, Marie thought, at least she had a fifty-five per cent chance not to fall ill again; this was the only way to look at it.

Surgery had been reassuring. Being injected with poison was not. She, who until now had felt no fear, this time was frightened. The ordeal was not over yet. But what other choice did she have? There is a curious link between rebellion and survival. Refusing the treatment would have been madness, but she needed some way of rebelling against the system and its rules. She had been told not to drive for six weeks. Well, she was not going to comply. Four weeks had gone since the operation when, admittedly with the greatest care, she took her car and went to see Jean. 'I once drove with a broken arm,' Jean told her chuckling with mischievous sparks in her eyes. They laughed together, enjoying their complicity. She was back in the world of the living.

A little bit bruised but at last out of the medical bubble, she couldn't wait to find out how the play was going. Those last few weeks, she had kept it out of her thoughts, knowing that the show was in Sue's professional hands. Still, Marie didn't know what to expect when she came to the hall in London where the last rehearsal was taking place – the first night was in less than four days and she had no idea what had gone on during the last few weeks. Sue and the boys, as Sue called the actors, greeted her with the unobtrusive warmth the English are so good at. She was moved. Then the rehearsal began and, here in front of her eyes, Rumi and Shams came to life. The choreography between Ashley and Duncan worked beautifully and the words rose with all their power and freshness. Only Robin still looked uncomfortable. Marie was not surprised. He was used to playing long pieces at a time, his playing an act of devotion, a sacred offering, and here, he was constantly interrupted in his flow, asked to play sometimes only for a few seconds, at most for a minute. Also, the idea of being exposed to a large audience – a paying one at that – added to his unease. He wanted his playing to be pure, but that was the reason why Marie had wanted him in the first place. Sue, for her part, thought that his sighing and complaining had more to do with stage fright. 'In the end,' she said, 'he'll get over it.' One thing was certain: without music, the play would have been incomplete; even Robin by now recognized it. Thank God, she thought, Robin was not the kind to renege on his commitment. But he was upset. At some point, when he was told to shorten his playing, 'I wish I had not got involved,' he mumbled between his teeth. Was he angry or, as Sue believed, frightened? Probably both. She let the storm pass and the rehearsal continued. 'Once the performance has started, he'll be all right,' she said to Marie. The first night was in less than a week and Robin didn't flee.

May 1998

It was the night of the first performance. People were arriving. Jean was among them, accompanied by a friend who helped her walk down the few steps to the entrance. The room was filling up, and a few more chairs had to be fetched. In exchange for publicity, a carpet dealer Marie had recently met had lent two large rugs to decorate the space, and the room with its supporting columns had taken on the look of Ali Baba's cave.

The performance went beautifully. Far from making any blunders, Robin was beaming. He had never played so well and with such sensitivity. Marie noticed people wiping tears while she herself felt as if she was back in Konya. Rumi and Shams, their meeting and their unbearable separation, had come to life with such vividness that when the last words resonated, there was a long silence before people came back to their surroundings and found their breath. *'The weaning from this world wasn't it like fire? The pilgrims are gone and in reality this weaning was Light.'* Duncan was on his knees with Ashley standing next to him, gazing into space somewhere beyond the audience. Then an explosion of applause.

Marie, Sue, the actors and the musicians bowed. Friends came with praise and flowers. Later on, in the front room, Marie noticed Ashley talking to Jean who was waiting for her friend. She took a few steps towards them but was stopped by a woman who wanted her to sign a copy of her book. She quickly obliged. 'Without you, the play wouldn't have happened,' she heard Ashley saying to Jean as she at last approached them. She had told him that the sale of the book that Jean had financed had greatly helped to set up the play. She was glad he acknowledged it.

'You have exceeded yourself,' Jean said to Marie.

'Real teamwork,' Marie replied thinking that all of them had given their best, 'but,' she repeated what Ashley had just said, 'without you, nothing could have happened.' The shadow of a grin appeared on Jean's face. She wouldn't refuse thanks, but that was enough. There was no question of giving her a hug. Anyway, money was not really the key here. Money had made the book possible and now the play, but this was incidental. The real fuel had been the love she felt for Jean and Jean's calm and sober care for her. It was love that had diffused the shadows of Alex, and then the fall-out from her illness. They both knew it. There was no need to talk about it.

A small woman was coming up to them. She was wearing an Indian dress of bright colours. 'Excuse me,' she said. 'My name is Lesley. I'm from the Gurdjieff Society.' She paused, brushed an invisible fleck of dust from her dress. 'I was wondering; would it be possible to have your play in our hall?' She looked about fifty, her sharp, confident gaze contrasted with her very feminine appearance. Taken by surprise, Marie didn't respond immediately. 'Oh, I don't mean right now; perhaps in a year,' the woman quickly added. Overwhelmed by the evening – its success, the people flocking around her and the fatigue – Marie could hardly take in what Lesley was saying. 'We could meet in a week or two,' Lesley suggested. 'Yes, yes. That would be good.' They exchanged phone numbers.

Marie was not prepared for the shock that followed the performances. Everyone was gone. She felt abandoned. No one had warned her that, from one day to the next, the closeness, the sharing and the intensity would all have disappeared. Even when in the hospital, she was still part of a team, almost a family. She knew the rehearsals were continuing and going well. Sue had kept in touch. Duncan had sent her a card, and now, all of a sudden, the team, the family, was gone. Some letters arrived, thanking her, one from her dear old friend David, saying he was 'still dazzled and vastly heartened.' This was comforting but it didn't replace the sense of fulfilment and meaning that had infused the last months.

As the chemotherapy sessions continued, Marie felt that the energy she had found in setting up the play, and then later at seeing it night after night, started to leak. The treatment was exhausting even though, by now, she was less frightened. And when, one morning, as she was preparing to go to work, the hospital rang to say that her next session had to be postponed because her blood had not recovered, it all felt too much. Alex gone forever, her efforts to keep her life going, the cancer and now, week after week, poison being injected in her body. She looked at her hands, thinner, skin almost transparent. What were they doing to her? Had she been right to accept the treatment? And then, the thought that had insinuated itself from the day she'd been told about her illness: it was the shock of Alex's rejection that had triggered the cancer. 'Cancer is not a psychological illness,' the oncologist had replied to her suggestion that an emotional shock could have been at the root of it. Perhaps, she thought, but there were people whose hair turned white in one night after the sudden death of a son or a daughter. The doubt remained. Weren't body and soul inextricably mixed? Thoughts began to spiral. Now that Alex was gone forever, what was she left with? If she recovered from her illness, what did the future hold? Loneliness and a life without meaning? She let herself cry until words surged in her mind, *'Ask for help and it will be given. When the baby wants milk,'* Rumi says, *'it cries to his mother, and then she comes and gives him milk.'* It was like a comforting shadow spreading over her. No one was admonishing her to be strong, to carry the load all by herself. Prayer was praise, love and adoration, but Rumi was reminding her of God's tenderness. Calling for help was also prayer. She sat up and wiped her tears; words forming in her mind: 'Please help, I can't do it all by myself.' Again tears came to her eyes, but this time, they were tears of relief. God did care. *'Remember that when a man is thirsty,'* Rumi says again, *'the water is asking, where is the drinker?'* Yes, she only had to remember. She still had four chemotherapy sessions in front of her and, afterwards, weeks of radiotherapy. Her body would get weaker and weaker; and inevitably, she would again fall prey to fear and depression. But this time she must not forget to call for help.

October 1998

Her last session of radiotherapy was over. For six weeks, every week for half an hour, she had been lying alone in a sterilised room, under a metal monster that beamed invisible death rays into her body. She had not allowed her fear to take over, but as the weeks went on, had lost more weight and become weaker. Reluctant at first at having the treatment – radiotherapy, she believed, could do as much harm as good – she had accepted to go through it on the advice of a doctor friend: 'If it were my daughter, I wouldn't hesitate,' he'd said, 'I would have it done.' Then someone at the hospital, a woman doctor, had argued that if she didn't go through the treatment and if the cancer recurred she would be very angry with herself. The argument had won.

Now at last, except for regular check-ups with the oncologist, she was free from the hospital; back in her life. Six weeks after her operation, she had gone back to work on a part-time basis. She went to see Jean regularly; the book of quotations was selling well; she began to make plans with Sue for the play to be performed at the Gurdjieff Society.

But she needed to regain strength as well as some weight. She'd lost over ten pounds during the last few months. A friend had recommended an acupuncturist. This ancient science, Marie believed, could help neutralize the negative effects of both chemotherapy and radiotherapy. Only three years ago, after a bout of flu, a few sessions of acupuncture had quickly brought her back on her feet. It had felt miraculous.

And so on a rainy October morning, Marie knocked at the door of a white cottage stowed away in a cul-de-sac near Chalk Farm. The thin Vietnamese woman in a white coat who opened the door was Dr Mun Ching herself. No make-up, jet-black hair neatly pulled behind her ears, she invited Marie into a small office. 'What brings you here?' she asked after offering her a seat. Marie talked of the cancer, of the treatments she had gone through and of her loss of weight. The woman listened with attention, her gaze fixed on Marie who felt compelled to add, 'I sometimes think that the cancer was caused by the emotional shock I had two years ago. It was like an inner earthquake.' Dr Mun Ching looked calmly at Marie, her face expressionless. 'The cancer has done its job,' she added, 'it has gathered all the hurt and the harm.' She rubbed her hands one against the other as if getting rid of the least speck of dust that might have stuck to them. 'Now it's gone,' she said. Her comment was unexpected. This small Vietnamese woman was intimating that the pain, the humiliation, the anger, the worries, all that had consumed Marie for so long had been taken away, that they were gone forever. She found herself unable to speak but Dr Mun Ching was not waiting for a reply. She stood up and led Marie to the adjacent treatment room.

The procedure was nothing new: the taking of the pulse with all the fingers one wrist after another, the planting of needles, some Marie hardly felt, some that felt as heavy as lead, and then half an hour of silence. She left feeling that she had been fed with a measure of healing serenity.

For the next two months Marie went to see Mun Ching regularly. Her energy began to return. She didn't doubt that the cancer was gone for good. It was comforting to think, as Mun Ching had implied, that the tumour had gathered the hurt and the harm, and that once removed, so would be the hurt and damage. It didn't quite feel like that, though. The wound had begun to heal but the hurt still lingered.

Autumn 1998

The air was getting colder, the days shorter. Marie didn't like this time of year. But she was now free from the hospital, from all the treatments. She could look forward to some rest at last.

It was just after five and she was to switch on the light when the phone rang. Her sister was not calling from Paris but from Lyon. Their mother was ill and it was serious. She was to be operated on by the end of the week. Marie must come. It was hard to believe. She was allowed no respite. The next morning she took an early Eurostar. A rapid change in Paris from the Gare du Nord to the Gare de Lyon and a few hours later, she and her sister were on the road to the hospital. The operation was due in two days time. Or so they thought, as that same evening the hospital rang: their mother had suffered peritonitis during the night; she was to be operated on that same day.

They waited several hours before it was over. 'The operation went well,' the surgeon said reassuringly, 'but,' he warned, 'we'll keep her in intensive care for a few days; the risk is not over.'

Only one person at a time was allowed in the intensive care unit. Plastic covers over her shoes, a sterilised coat over her clothes, Marie tiptoed into the room. Her mother's face was drawn, eyes still misty from the anaesthetics, but she was conscious; she managed a faint smile but was too weak to speak. The next day when Marie came back, she was wide awake. At the sight of Marie, she raised a hand to her mouth to indicate she wanted to speak. Marie bent over the bed and stroked her hand. 'I want you to forgive me,' her mother murmured. Marie started. She didn't expect this. 'I have not given you a good idea of marriage,' her mother continued. 'I'm sorry.' Marie shook her head, tears blurring her vision. 'Please, there is nothing to forgive. You did all you could. I love you.' She left the room, her heart pounding. So her mother hadn't forgotten that remark of hers, years ago when, unable to commit herself, Marie had broken her engagement. Why couldn't Marie do as everyone else did and get married? her mother had complained. 'Well, you gave me a strange idea of marriage,' Marie had retorted. Her mother had left the room without a word. They had never talked about it again. So many times as a child, Marie had heard her mother asserting that marriage was no better than imprisonment. The bitterness of those remarks, the stuffiness in their home, the lack of air! But of course, it was not air that was lacking, it was love.

After a week, her mother recovered. Now out of intensive care, after a couple of weeks at the hospital she would be transferred to a convalescent home, and then soon could return home. Life could resume its course.

Spring 1999

The first daffodils were appearing in the parks when *Love's Journey* was performed at the Gurdjieff Society, this time with an internationally renowned *ney* player. Again, it drew a large audience and was a success. At the end, when a man came to Marie and introduced himself as a Benedictine monk, she was not really surprised. 'I want this in my Abbey,' he said. The next year – by now it was early 2000 – *Love's Journey* was performed within the walls of Douai Abbey, a magnificent monastery some thirty miles west of London, in which classic architecture fused seamlessly with the new in the same praise of God. That night, though, when, the words, La ilaha illa Allah rose between these very Christian walls, Marie felt a shudder passing through the audience, that only subsided when Duncan added, giving the Arabic words their meaning, 'God is the only Reality.'

During that same period, Marie read about a young girl called Kimya in a book on the life of Rumi. While still a child, the book said, she had been taken into his household and had grown up within his family. There were only a few lines about her and only, it seemed, because she had married Shams, Rumi's friend and teacher. She had died at an early age and, according to the gossip of the time, had been miserable, kept more or less locked in, due to Shams' jealousy. Somehow the story didn't feel right. There was more to Kimya, Marie felt, than this banal account. Brought up by Rumi, married to Shams, the child must have been special. Almost three years ago, during that first visit to the village, Marie had taken a photograph of a child no more than eight years old. She had placed it on top of her desk, a reminder of the beauty of the village and its people. She looked at the photograph. Here was Kimya smiling at her in all her sweetness, innocence and trust. Marie's imagination took flight. This was the child growing next to these two great men and soon to become a woman, and she, Marie, had to put her story on paper. It took her less than a week; the story was writing itself and it wanted to be published. The magazine that specialised in Sufism, where she submitted it, accepted it immediately. When she gave a copy to Margaret, her reaction took her aback. 'This story,' Margaret said, 'deserves more than a few pages. The characters, the time, the whole background deserve a book.' She, writing a book! It would never have crossed her mind. But other people thought the same. The story asks to be developed, they said; it needs to be expanded into a novel.

Marie was not so sure. The task was intimidating. Hardly anything was known about Kimya. And how does one write a book? Several weeks passed. She kept thinking of Kimya. In her short story, Rumi had adopted Kimya after her parents had died in an accident. This seemed too simplistic. An inner truth suggested that Kimya had come from a village in the Taurus Mountains. A village like Mehmet's village, a village where an eight year old looks at the world with wide, trusting eyes! 'If you ever want to spend some time in the village,' Mehmet had said, 'you tell me and I will organize it.' This was it. She would go and live there for a while and get to know Kimya and her surroundings.

It was soon agreed: Marie could come any time this summer. It would be hot in Turkey, she surmised, but in the mountains –

the village, Mehmet had once told her, was at almost six thousand feet above sea level – it would be pleasant.

July 1999 – The village

It was late July when she arrived in Konya, almost three years since her last visit. Nothing much had changed. As in the previous years, she took a room at the Dergah then went to the shop where Mehmet and Muammer greeted her as if she had never left. She had brought a copy of her book of quotations, which she gave to Muammer. He was learning Persian, he had told her, and she suspected he wrote poetry. Obviously pleased, he leafed through the book, read a line and smiled at her. 'Thank you. I will look after it,' he said.

'We drive to the village tomorrow,' interrupted Mehmet. He had organized everything for Marie's stay. 'You will be with a good family. I arranged with them.'

Once again as the road wound its way up, she was overwhelmed by the beauty and vastness of the landscape. At times, as the car took a sharp turn, it seemed as if they were taking off into the blue of the sky. After an hour, she recognized the cluster of houses the same ochre and reddish colour as the earth, clinging to the slope, about a mile away. 'Here is the village,' confirmed Mehmet. Her family, he said, consisted of a couple and their three daughters. 'They have electricity and a shower room,' Mehmet added, no doubt a luxury in the village. Kimya wouldn't have known any of this. Was this cheating? Marie shrugged the thought away. She was glad this was not the thirteenth century.

Two minutes later, they reached the first houses. Already, a bunch of children were running towards them shrieking and waving, and people began to appear and cheer. Two women washing grapes at the fountain waved and smiled at them before returning to their task. Mehmet nodded in the direction of a small one-storey cube of stones and mud supported by rough wooden beams. This was to be her home for the next seven days. The base of the house stretched into a terrace – actually the roof of the stable that, underneath, sheltered a donkey and a few goats. The family were sitting drinking tea. The man, who was wearing a bright green shirt, took a few steps to the short ladder at the corner of the roof, and held his hand to help them reach the terrace. The rest of the family waited with expectant smiles. As she approached, Marie stretched her hand, but the large woman, probably in her forties but already worn by hard work, took her in her arms. The girls kissed her on both cheeks. The father shook her hand. They all sat down and one of the girls went to fetch some more tea. It was time for the presentations. Mehmet gave her name then the mother pointed at her youngest daughter, short hair and no scarf. 'This is Aysel, she is nine,' Mehmet translated, 'she still goes to school.' Aysel, grinned, showing all her teeth. A cheeky little one, Marie thought; she looked quite a handful. 'It's her last year at school,' Mehmet said. 'After that, there is no more education, unless she goes to Konya, but,' he shrugged, 'they don't have the money.' And this is Gizem,' Mehmet went on. 'She is fifteen.' Gizem nodded but remained stern. Her sister, Esma, the eldest, a beautiful young woman with dark gazelle eyes, was eighteen. She gave a quick smile, and then stood up to fill more glasses of tea. Having done his duty, Mehmet turned to the husband and began chatting with him while the girls and their mother, four smiling faces, looked at Marie. After a few minutes, the mother said something but Marie shook her head and the woman gave up. What did they think? To them she could just as well have fallen from the moon. After a while, the mother pointed at herself. 'Hatije,' she said, 'Hatije.' The husband interrupted his discussion with Mehmet, and laughing he turned towards Marie and pointed a finger at his chest. 'Zia, Baba,' then went back to his discussion. Marie couldn't help laughing too. Her hand on her chest, she said, 'Me, Marie.' Hatije and the girls kept smiling. Marie hid a sigh.

Without Mehmet, it was not going to be easy to communicate. He had told her how much her staying with the family meant to them. 'You see, the villagers have no cash. They grow their food but that's all. With your paying for your stay, they'll be able to buy a few things, like a pair of shoes for Aysel or candles. In winter,' he added, 'because of the snow, candles are precious.' She understood. There were often power cuts when the snow brought down the electric lines. Yes, these people were poor and the sum agreed was ridiculously low. But again, the light in their eyes; this light didn't lie. In spite of the poverty, they were content with their lives.

With Mehmet gone, time slowed. Night was falling and they all went inside. Hatije and the two older daughters disappeared in the kitchen to prepare dinner, leaving Marie with Aysel and Baba in what appeared to be both living room and dining room. Sitting against the wall facing Marie, Baba grinned at her awkwardly. Aysel said something, but once again, powerless, Marie shook her head. Her few basic Turkish words were not sufficient. She began to wonder whether it had been such a good idea to come and spend seven long days with people whose language she didn't share, in conditions that could only be called primitive. Boredom was going to be hard to bear. Aysel had gone out of the room and returned with a piece of paper and a red pencil. She sat down, and, lips tight with concentration, began to write a few words then presented the paper to Marie who read the words CHILD and AYSEL. Amused, Marie nodded. 'Yes, Aysel, you're a child. That's very, very good.' Beaming with pride, Aysel showed the piece of paper to her father whose grin broadened. Reading and writing, Marie suspected, were not his main concerns in life, but he certainly was proud of his clever daughter.

At that moment, Hatije and the two other girls came in the room carrying a large steaming pot. Esma had already spread the *sofre*, a piece of fabric that served as tablecloth, on the floor then, taking the pot from her mother, she placed it in the middle. From a plastic bag, Hatije took out a handful of thin paper-like bread, which she tore apart and passed around. Then, armed with a spoon, everyone sat around and picked into the stew, a mixture of potatoes, tomatoes and beans, which Marie found really tasty. Did they eat like this all the time, she wondered, or was this especially for her? She looked around. They were picking at the food with their spoon, and then mopped up the sauce with the bread. Simple and easy, she thought, and no plates and hardly any cutlery to wash afterwards.

Before everybody retired, Hatije brought two large thick cushions – her mattress – plus two sheets and a light blanket. So the room was to be Marie's bedroom. From the size of the house, she suspected that the whole family was going to sleep in the room next door; there didn't seem to be any other room. She would have the luxury of this one all to herself. She could have shared with one of the daughters; but no, she was the guest, and anyhow, both of them would have been embarrassed.

Her watch said eight when Marie woke the next morning; she wondered how long the rest of the household had been up. It was surprising how well she had slept. Life in the village probably followed the rhythm of the sun, which at this time of year meant early rise and late set. She was not quite up to it yet. She could hear people talking in the room next door, and outside, the strident crow of a rooster mingling with the bells of goats on their way to pasture, and the obstinate braying of a donkey. She pulled the curtain. A few yards away, next to the mosque, the minaret rose against the blue of the sky. On the horizon, the mountain ranges stretched in the morning haze. Perhaps it was their soundless majesty that had permeated her sleep. Still, the call to prayer should have woken her and yet she had slept well after dawn, unlike in Konya where, just before daybreak, the first calls to prayer always started her out of sleep. Had the villagers asked the muezzin to keep his call to himself or at least to keep it discreet? This was not unlikely. These people in their simplicity and self-confidence possessed a large dose of common sense, something she thought urban sophistication was lacking. She shook herself. They certainly didn't expect her to spend the morning in bed. She quickly dressed and was piling up sheets, blanket and cushions when, framed in the door, Hatije's big smile appeared, with, behind her, Esma carrying a tray with a small teapot, glasses and a bowl of yoghourt. She managed a quick cold shower and returned to find that, like the night before, the *sofre* had been spread on the floor. She sat on a cushion; Hatije distributed torn sheets of bread around and Gizem brought a large aluminium container with a small tap on top, a sort of samovar filled with hot water. A moment later, Baba came with a jar of dark, thick honey. Marie couldn't have wished for a better breakfast. Afterwards, she helped the women clear up but was sent away from the kitchen, reminded again that guests were not supposed to work. Aysel was waiting for her in what was now the sitting room, the small English/Turkish dictionary Marie had noticed earlier on the windowsill in her hands. She handed it to Marie. Why had she not thought of bringing one herself? *'Teshekur*, Aysel.' The word for thank you was about the only one she knew. Turkish, unrelated as it was to any European language, and with its constant use of suffixes and prefixes, seemed like a nightmare. She had never attempted to learn it. Aysel was pointing at herself, 'Girl.' Marie couldn't help laughing. 'Yes, you, girl,' she said, somehow impressed that in this remote Turkish village a child was so keen to learn another language. It put her to shame. Hatije was back, and with much smiling and gesturing indicated that there were other things to do than looking at books. They were going out to pick some fruit and vegetables. Each family had its small plot of land, Marie learnt, but did share a lot with each other. The village was more or less self-sufficient, its life mostly centred round the fountain. It was there in the long stone tub that the water channelled from the mountains ended up for the women to wash the wheat, the vegetables, the grapes. It was at the fountain that women and children came to fetch water and exchange the latest gossip, and there that, twice a day, the animals – sheep, goats, donkeys, mules and even a few cows – were taken to drink. And it was by the fountain that the women did their washing. Marie saw two of them one morning beating clothes on a flat stone with a mallet, and next to them, a huge black cauldron resting above a small fire of twigs, from which emerged clouds of steam that swirled around the women. On the backdrop of the mountains, with the sun filtering above them, the scene had a dreamlike quality. Yet, as Marie was well aware, the hands of the women might have told a different story.

As the days went by, Marie began to see that what she found picturesque was simply poverty. This didn't mean unhappiness, though. The children, who took part in everything, helped and played at the same time so that work often took the colour of a game. A walk along the stream that ran beside a curtain of poplars led to picking plums, tomatoes, cucumbers and peppers. Nibbling seeds was fun while gathering them from the heart of the sunflowers withering in the sun. One morning, as Marie walked towards the end of the village, she discovered on top of a hill a couple and two horses threshing wheat. The horses were harnessed to a small platform on which the woman was standing holding the reins. They walked in circles, pulling a heavy wooden plank studded with stones and sharp pieces of metal that crushed the ears of wheat as they clumped along. Behind them, the man tossed the grain in the air to get rid of the chaff while a bunch of children took turns to ride the plank as a merry-go-round.

Early another morning, as she looked through the window, Marie caught sight of Hatije stirring piles of yellow grains in one of those vast cauldrons set on top of a wood fire. She remembered their collecting wood earlier during a walk in the wood nearby.

Outside, the air was filled with a smell that reminded her of baked bread or of a cake just taken out of the oven. Hatije was cooking wheat, which the children – no one stopped them – picked by the handfuls and stuffed in their mouths. Marie soon discovered that everyone in the village was busy doing the same. Once cooked, the grain was spread on the roof terraces and left to dry until the next morning. As night fell, the wheat was covered with fabric and stones were placed at each corner to hold it. The next day in the afternoon, she joined a group of women on one of the roofs where they were sorting out scraps of dirt from piles of dry wheat, by then as hard as stone. This was bulgur, she realized, the same crushed dry cooked wheat used in taboule, the Middle Eastern salad she had often ordered in Lebanese restaurants in London. She watched one of the women standing up with a full basket of wheat in her hands, which she raised as high as she could, and whose contents she tipped for the wind to blow the chaff away. Another of those timeless scenes that stayed in Marie's memories: the bright colours of the women's dresses, the chatting and laughing, the play of sun and shadows on their faces. Encircling them the mountain ranges stretching under a sky peppered with small, white clouds. It struck her that there was not the least trace of self-consciousness in these women or any desire to be somewhere else.

The light was turning gold and the wheat was ready to be packed. A group of young men had just appeared as if from nowhere. They were bringing large bags made of cloth, which the women quickly filled with the wheat. They threw the bags over their shoulders and carried them down to the communal silo. The day's work was over. As the sun sank behind the Taurus, the women dispersed. Not for a minute had Marie thought of Alex. She was not sure whether this made her happy or sad.

And so passed the days. The disorientation, the feeling of being trapped, even the boredom, had gone. Hatije and Baba seemed more like family; the girls more like sisters. The daily process of surviving, often through harsh conditions, gave life its rhythm and its meaning. No need here for extra entertainment, no loneliness either as the concept of privacy seemed not to exist. There was no doubt these people were content with their lives, but they certainly wouldn't have refused the convenience of the modern water closet or of the washing machine; those were simply out of reach and, so, there was no point in desiring them. Nor would Esma, the eldest daughter who suffered from a toothache, have refused to see a dentist. It just didn't occur to her as the family couldn't afford it, and anyway, any dentist was at least two hours away.

It was not only Marie who had adapted. Hatije and her family too had adjusted to their guest and her incomprehensible need for solitude. They now knew that when Marie took her notebook, she wanted to be left alone. She used those moments to keep her diary. At times, she pretended to read her book of Sufi stories. But this respecting of her solitude didn't extend beyond the limits of the village. Whenever she tried to go for a walk on her own, Gizem appeared by her side. One evening, as Marie ventured off-limits to enjoy the sunset over the mountains, Gizem was on her heels. She gestured to her to go away, to leave her alone. The girl's only concession was to stand at a short distance and watch Marie looking at the sky. What crossed her mind? Marie wondered; nothing probably. Foreigners were simply foreign, there was no point trying to understand.

Her stay was coming to an end. In two days, the weekly bus to Konya would bring her back to the twentieth century. In the end, Marie had not really suffered from boredom; she had not missed much of her modern life either. It would feel strange at first to be back; she would miss the village and its people, their warmth, their simplicity, though the comforts Westerners take so easily for granted would be welcomed. Sharing the toilet with a goat and a calf or showering without hot water was not particularly enjoyable. And being free to go anywhere without someone watching her every move would be a relief. Of course, freedom and individuality have their price: indifference, anonymity, loneliness. But none of them had any choice. She could no more live the way her ancestors had than Hatije and Zia could jump into the twentieth century.

She was lost in her thoughts when Baba came in and, pointing outside, indicated they were going for a walk. Aysel and Gizem were coming too. Zia ahead, they took a path that wound up its way out of the village through an arid land of grass and stones. After a while, bushes appeared, several of them with small round leaves that glistened in the sun. As they passed by them, Baba tore off large handfuls of foliage, with which he rapidly filled a bag. Aysel pointed at the bag and, her eyes fixed on Marie, mimicked the braying of the donkey. They all laughed. 'Yes, I understand,' said Marie, 'this is fodder for the donkey.'

It was getting hot and the bag was full; time to turn back, Marie thought. But Zia had something else in mind, and instead continued down a red earth valley then, once at the bottom, turned abruptly to the left and began climbing again until they arrived at a plateau. There were no obvious marks or signposts but Zia seemed to know his way, and he continued walking with determination. Tired, sweating, the drone of insects in her ears, her feet stung by countless thistles her sandals didn't quite protect from, Marie was beginning to feel irritated. She was thinking of sitting down in protest when, among the sea of high grass swaying in the breeze, she saw that Zia had stopped. He made a sign for her to come closer. She took a few steps and there in front of her eyes, rooted in the earth and reminiscent of a tombstone, stood a large slab of white marble. She bent down. Carved in relief on the stone, a small cavalier on his horse, a bell in one hand, a banner in the other, was waving at her from the past. Her travel guide talked of the period of 'Hellenized Anatolia' and dated it back to about 300 BC. She knew, of course, that civilizations had come and gone on this land, leaving their mark along the centuries, but she had not expected to find traces of those civilizations among the hills of the Taurus, far away from the large centre of Constantinople or even from Konya. How many men and women and children had lived or passed through here? Zia was pressing her to walk further. This time it was to show her a carved lion, lying on its head, part of its body missing. Zia knew each of the stones. Another few steps and here, half hidden in the dry grass, he showed Marie a piece of marble engraved this time with a cross inside a circle and, further along, another stone with the same design. Were these the remains of a church? Then she was wrong about her dates. At her feet, scattered around, were pieces of pottery. People had lived here. The place felt like an abandoned graveyard. Centuries ago, the old Greco-Roman world had reached as far as these mountains. Apparently, no archaeologist had bothered to explore this stretch of ancient land or cared about what it held. Historians and archaeologists had enough places to dig and material to study in more accessible areas in the Middle East.

Zia was moving ahead. Stepping over a clump of thistles, she joined him in front of a slab larger than the previous ones. This one had no motif, only a long inscription in Greek letters, written without any space between the words. To a scholar, this would have helped to date the inscription but Marie was no scholar and she didn't read Greek. All she could tell was that the inscription belonged to Byzantine times. Was that before Rumi or when he lived in Konya? She suddenly felt caught in a spiral of time. Could it be that Kimya had really lived here at the time? Marie took several photographs of the stones. Perhaps someone in London could date them.

Two days later, she boarded the rickety bus for Konya. A last hug from Hatije, a last handshake with Zia, kisses from the girls, and in a cloud of red dust, the village disappeared behind the mountains. As the bus entered the plain of Konya, she felt a mixture of sadness and relief. She was glad to get back to modern life and its comfort, but feared that the taste of peace and simple enjoyment that she had experienced in the village was soon to evaporate. At least, Kimya's first years were now more tangible.

Paris 2014

It is fifteen years since her stay in the village, and only now does it hit her that it had been much more than an exotic and useful parenthesis. A retreat, no doubt, it had taken her out of her ordinary life and her obsession with Alex, while giving her a lot of material for her book. What she had not expected - and not been aware of at the time - was that that short week spent with Hatije and her family had re-delineated her values. Her mind knew nothing of it, but in a concrete and physical way, she had discovered that the very meaning of life was in living itself. 'You don't know when you are learning,' Bruce, the hippy psychotherapist who, some forty years ago, had introduced her to Sufism, had once told her. What he had not told her was that it takes time for wisdom to take roots. Once more, she marvelled at the invisible hand guiding her steps.

November 1999

Marie was just back from Turkey when her sister phoned to tell her the news. Though their mother was still at home, officially convalescing, she was weakening. Marie and her sister continued to alternate their visits, Chantal from Paris, Marie from London. Once again the battle between life and death was engaged and no one knew which side was to win.

It was on her return from one of her trips to France that Marie received a phone call. Jean had passed away two days earlier while Marie was still abroad: a cold that had turned into pneumonia, which, in a few days, had carried her off. She had died in hospital and was to be buried the next day. There would be no ceremony – Jean didn't care for what she called the fuss of religion – and her body would rest in an unmarked grave among trees in a non-consecrated part of a cemetery near Richmond. No one would ever be able to detect where she had been buried. Faithful to her convictions, Jean had also made clear that there wouldn't be any waste of money on a traditional coffin; hers was to be made of green cardboard. She had come and gone; there would be no traces left of her having been on this earth, except, as all those present that day at her funeral would have claimed, in the hearts of the many who had benefited from her unsentimental, fierce knowledge.

It was difficult to judge how many people were there. Hundreds it seemed; among them, Michael whom Marie had not seen for a while. She had no idea that he too knew Jean. With his milky, freckled skin and eyebrows so blond they were almost invisible, he was the typical Norman. In spite of his small frame, his strong masculine presence was comforting. Tears swelling in her eyes, her lips quivering, she fell into his arms, too upset to talk. He let her sob on his shoulder until she calmed down and they could talk. He had met Jean two years ago, only a few times, he said, but had remained grateful for her helping him find a better balance. 'She was special,' he said. Marie nodded. With Jean gone, her last anchor had been taken away. Another chapter was closing. 'Yes,' she said, 'we were privileged to know her.'

In the weeks that followed, she made herself sit every day at her computer, Jean's voice still ringing in her ear, 'Are you writing?' and refused to listen to the voice pressing her to clear her wardrobe or try that latest recipe. She couldn't let Jean down.

March 2000

Two months after Jean's passing, Chantal called again. It had taken four months for fate to make itself known. Their mother's health had badly deteriorated; she had just been admitted in a small country hospital outside Lyon; Chantal was calling from there. 'You must come,' her sister said. She added that, at this point, the doctors could do nothing except stem the pain. The news, though predictable, was still a shock. 'There is little time left,' Chantal added. 'The doctors don't give her more than a few days, perhaps less.' She choked on the last words, then, 'Let me know what time you will arrive. I'll pick you up at the airport.'

The room is no more than a square white box; its window looks over a patch of ploughed earth dotted with yellow blobs of forsythia. In this small white space, a life is ebbing away. They are all here, the three of them, Marie standing on one side of the bed, her sister sitting on the other side, their brother at the foot of the bed. Their mother wants to speak and Marie bends over. 'I didn't take care of you properly,' her mother says. It is as if two hands were squeezing Marie's heart, pressing the blood out of it. 'You did the best you could,' she replies. 'That's all you could do.' Her mother shakes her head, 'I shouldn't have had that affair, I…' She is out of breath and pauses. Marie holds the tears that blur her vision. 'You were looking for love,' she says. 'You were looking for intensity.' Her mother nods and closes her eyes. She seems relieved; someone understands. 'You got confused,' Marie continues. 'You fixed all that desire on a man.' Without opening her eyes, her mother nods again. 'I did the same with Alex,' Marie adds. 'I too got confused.' The words spring out, soothing, healing words. 'It doesn't matter. All that matters is how much you've loved.' Her mother keeps her eyes closed but the slight frown on her forehead signals that she is not asleep. 'And now you are going towards that love, that intensity.' Her mother's face has softened; her breathing now calm and regular. Marie stands. There is no more to say. The three of them tiptoe out of the room.

Hours later, lying in bed between wakefulness and sleep, Marie gasps: the words she had spoken to her mother were aimed at herself too. They had sprung as if someone – Rumi? – had dictated them. She had been the voice transmitting a message intended for them both. Grief and gratitude make a strange mix.

While grieving at her mother's dying, she was at the same time grateful for having been able to bring her peace, grateful too at the depth of their connection.

When the phone rang, waking her up, it was no surprise. 'Your mother has just died,' said the voice of the nurse. Death had struck as sharp as a sword, dropping on her a cloak of numbness. On the bedside table the clock said five-thirty. She got up and went to wake her sister.

Dawn breaking over the countryside, patches of yellow forsythias emerging from the night, the long grey ribbon of the road, making its way through the fields. In the silence, the purr of the car engine. Each of them lost in her personal grief. One after the other, Marie's bridges are being burnt behind her. At least, that's how it feels. There is no going back. More than ten years ago, she had felt sadness at her father's death but curiously she didn't really miss him. It was more as if he had gone somewhere abroad and that both of them were content to live their lives miles apart. This time, it is different. Thoughts like piercing arrows keep hitting her: never to hear her mother's voice again, never to laugh or quarrel with her, never to confide in her, never to phone her or receive a letter from her. A last turn, and the small country hospital appears on top of the hill. They emerge from the car; large glass doors slid open in front of them, narrow lift to the second floor, blank silence. Strange how facing death feels like being washed. An ancient Tibetan prayer comes to her mind: I have no father, Thou art my father – I have no mother, Thou art my mother... The rest of the prayer eludes her except for its last words, I go to the Spirit of the Void, and I go, and I go, and I go: an emptying of everything leading towards that deep longing which can't be named.

London – 2000

How does one live one's life as it is being made empty? Back in London, back at her writing, the only way to survive was to keep busy. Almost in spite of her, Kimya's story was beginning to take shape. The memories of the village were still vivid: the washing of the wheat, the making of bulgur, the mountain ranges around the village, the people's faces, it all became part of the story. But still, writing in English, a language she was far from mastering, seemed insane. At times, she cut herself short from lack of words, lack of ease. One day, she stopped; tomorrow I'll get back to it, she told herself. Then tomorrow, and tomorrow again. It was simpler to lose oneself in research. There was a mass of information about life in Konya at the time of Rumi: the trade between Venice and the East, the enlightened Sultan who surrounded himself with men of knowledge and wisdom, the crumbling of Byzantium and the advance of the Turkish tribes, and then the Mongol invasion. Hypnotized by her readings, she kept away for months from her computer, only glancing at it from time to time, with a feeling of guilt. Yet, one day, almost to her surprise, Kimya's story started to unfold. She had now arrived in Konya and entered Rumi's household; she was beginning to learn Persian and, through a kind of osmosis, as if the centuries had become porous, Marie registered at the School of Oriental and African Studies and started a course in Persian. And when the original words of Rumi became alive with meaning, Kimya was looking over her shoulder, whispering the words Marie was deciphering. This didn't make her writing any easier, though. Being a student and working part time didn't leave much space to write. She wondered: would she ever finish her novel? At times, the task felt beyond her. At least, she had little space to brood over Alex. She prayed and asked for help. And unexpectedly, it came, in the shape of a dream.

The Dream

Suspended in stillness, a woman and a man locked in space face each other, fingers barely touching in a faint suggestion of God bringing life to Adam on the ceiling of the Sistine Chapel. The woman is full of apprehension and fear. 'I can't,' she says, hardly able to breathe, 'I can't.'

'Yes, you can,' he calmly replies. With his hands he makes a spherical shape and repeats, 'You can, but not for me, for all of us.' Her breathing begins to ease, fear melts away; she takes hold of his hand and together they begin to dance in space in perfect harmony. It is glorious. The feeling of completeness – the same feeling she'd experienced with Alex in Paris – is so intense that she wakes up.

She sat for a while on her bed, overwhelmed, the energy of the dream still running through her veins. A thought surged, more of an insight: it was not Alex she had been missing and grieving for; it was this feeling of completeness; it was the experience of wholeness of which Alex had been the vehicle. But without him, would she ever be able to contact this energy again? Tears came to her eyes. Yet a sense of relief was taking over mixed with a new certainty: she would finish her book.

For weeks, the dream resonated with subtle and precise implications, its message and symbolism inexhaustible: she was on her way to re-own that masculine part of herself she had projected on Alex. She now possessed the strength to write her book. But the dream also contained a warning: her writing was not for the satisfaction of her ego; it was to help her become whole.

It took Marie five more months to complete her novel, and then to have her English checked by a friend. After that, all she could do was ask for more help. 'You made me write this book,' she prayed. 'You must now help me find a publisher.' And the miracle happened. Of the two publishers she had contacted, one accepted her manuscript and offered her a contract. The first bursts of colour above the garden fence came at the same time as the choosing of a cover. Spring was on its way. In a few weeks, the wisteria would display its annual extravaganza of scented blue. And finally, in the heat of summer, her novel would start its life on the shelves of bookshops. Four month to wait, the perfect opportunity to go to Konya.

May 2001

As last time – almost three years ago – it was just after sunset when her taxi deposited her in front of the Dergah. It was as if time had shrunk. Immediately, this feeling of being home. But as Rumi would have said, 'Where is home if not in the heart?' and right now, her heart didn't want to be anywhere else. Yet, she thought, she would never be able to live in Konya. She stopped herself; this swirling of thoughts was useless. Still standing on the pavement in front of the hotel, she decided to go and see Mehmet before checking in. At this time of year, there would be plenty of rooms available.

There was only Muammer in the shop. He greeted her with the same sweet welcome as ever. A minute later, sitting among the carpets, she was drinking tea as if she had never left. He sat next to her and asked, 'Do you know Alex…' he mispronounced the surname but there was no doubt, he was talking about the only Alex she knew. She put her glass down; her hand shaking, her mind gone blank. 'He was here last week,' Muammer continued. 'I showed him your book.' Alex here!… In this shop! A week ago! Muammer's words kept echoing. How was it that of all the carpet shops in Konya, Alex had chosen this rather shabby one hidden in a side street when there were many more attractive shops on the main road? And he had held her book in his hands! Muammer had gone silent. 'You know him?' he asked.

'Yes, I used to,' Marie said. 'But we are not in touch anymore.' Muammer nodded and kept silent. Why did their paths have to cross? She took a long sip at her tea and tried to smile. Alex was not to spoil her stay in Konya. 'Where is Mehmet?' she asked. Mehmet was in Istanbul, on a business trip, but he would be back the next day. They chatted for a while; Alex was not mentioned again. Still, she couldn't keep him out of her thoughts. What had he made of her book? The book, he would have known, which they were supposed to have written together. The day suddenly weighed on her. She had arrived in Turkey through Izmir in the middle of the night the day before, slept a few hours, and caught the coach to Konya, the journey hardly shorter than from Istanbul. Her tiredness didn't escape Muammer. 'I'll take you to your hotel,' he said, picking up her bag.

She found her room unchanged and fell asleep immediately. Just before dawn, woken up by the call to prayer echoing over the city, the wave of love that enfolded her was as familiar as her room. The first daylight began filtering through the curtain and with it, the ghost of Alex dissolved.

August 2004

It was summer when the novel was finally published and when, from the solitary corner of Marie's sitting room, Kimya emerged into the world. The book sold immediately and soon reached Indonesia, Turkey, Serbia, then the Gulf States and India... It went on being translated into several languages, though not into French, so, most of Marie's family were unable to read it. She received letters and emails that thanked her for 'having made my heart sing again,' 'for having helped me out of depression,' 'for the nourishment it gave me...'

She could still hear Jean's voice admonishing her to write. Wherever Jean now was, she would be pleased. She would be even more pleased to see Marie standing on her own two feet, free from her entanglement with Alex. Never again would she fall under the spell of another human being. It had been a hard lesson to learn but 'who ever promised you that life would be a bed of roses?' These were the words Doris Lessing kept repeating to herself in her autobiography. They made Marie smile. Yes, it was painful but why be so indignant when life makes you grow up?

Jerusalem – Summer 2014

She was back in that same square of almost twenty years ago. The jacaranda tree was still there, not much bigger than last time and still casting its shade, this time over an old man sitting on the wall nearby. She had just finished drinking a glass of carrot juice in that same café where she'd sat in 1994. Nothing seemed to have changed: the tables and chairs set up in the corner opposite the tree were still inviting the passers-by to stop for refreshment. No little RezaLeah in sight this time though, and Gedaliah had moved to another quarter 'Nachlaot,' he'd told her yesterday on the phone. She had the precise address but couldn't orientate herself in the labyrinth of the Old City. Perhaps the man coming towards her knew.

'Where is the Nachlaot quarter?' The man seemed to be in a hurry.

'Who are you looking for?' he asked.

'A rabbi,' she answered mechanically, aware that in the Old City the number of rabbis by square miles probably exceeded half the population. The man didn't seem surprised.

'Which rabbi?' he immediately asked.

'Gedaliah F…' she said, wondering why the question. Did everybody here carry in his head the list of all the rabbis in Jerusalem?

Without hesitation, the man said, 'He doesn't live here anymore.' And then as if remembering her question, 'Nachlaot is not in Old Jerusalem. It's about half a mile away.' He left her disconcerted. She needed to phone Gedaliah again.

Gedaliah had not changed much. Perhaps he had gained a little more weight, a few more wrinkles, but he still radiated the same goodness and serenity of years ago. They sat quietly in a small room which seemed to serve as much as an office as a sitting room. 'How are you?' he asked, and before she could reply, he added, 'You know you can ask me any question you want.' She couldn't help a smile.

'I'm well,' she said. She felt content. To ask him questions? She searched her mind in vain. She had none. So they sat together chatting about everything and nothing, like two good friends, happy to share each other's company.

'Would you like a glass of water?' he asked after a while and she gladly accepted. It was early afternoon; outside, the sun was beating hard and in Gedaliah's small flat, in spite of the window open on the greenness of a courtyard, the heat was stifling. Left to herself, she reflected how much he had been a part of her journey even though, during all those years, they had not seen each other more than half a dozen times. He'd been the first to guide her through the storm that had engulfed her almost twenty years ago. Then they had met a few more times in London when, after his stays in America, he came and offered his spiritual teaching on the Kabbalah, which he illustrated with Hassidic tales. She still believed that she owed him her life. Not that she would have actively put an end to it, but at the time when she was letting herself drift towards self-destruction – and he was probably aware of it – he had been the only light on her path. 'Thank you,' she said as he came back with the glass of water, and placed it on the desk next to her.

'How long are you staying in Jerusalem?' he asked as he sat down.

'Only a week, I arrived two days ago. So I won't see you much, but I'll come another time to say goodbye.'

'Oh! No.' He was shaking his head. 'I want to see you every day,' he paused, '... except Saturday, of course.' She was taken by surprise. He didn't seem to expect a reply; it was tacitly agreed. They then talked about her life in England, his recent marriage with a woman whose son found it difficult to accept his mother's remarriage.

'It will take time,' Gedaliah said philosophically. They talked about simple things like the traditional market a few yards away that, he said, she should visit, about his search for a larger place to live. Nothing forced, even their silent pauses when, empty of thoughts, she looked through the window at the dusty trees weighed down by the heat. She must have stayed an hour or more; time with Gedaliah had a way of stretching.

'Come tomorrow,' he said as he took her to the door. 'Would two-thirty as today be all right?' She nodded. They might have nothing special to talk about but sitting with Gedaliah was like warming oneself at a fire. It was not to be refused.

As she left his house, it occurred to her that in coming to Jerusalem and visiting him she was putting the full stop on her story with Alex. After all those years, she still didn't know and would never know why he had pushed her out of his life, but this had little to do with her and didn't matter anymore. Alex had become a faded shadow. She had no doubt about it – and Gedaliah would agree – her encounter with him had been a blessing. Life, she thought, was like a series of coloured threads woven into patterns over an invisible weft – the Unseen world of the Sufis. From the human point of view, her encounter with Alex had made for a rather sad and unsolved story. But on the level of the soul, it was Alex who had opened her heart to Rumi, and then it was his rejection that had started her on her own inner quest. Everything had been and was as it should be. Alex had been the route to her journey to God. She could only be grateful.

Paris 2014

It had taken her some ten years to recover from her encounter with Alex. It had then taken her another ten years to digest it and look at it with a certain detachment. Now, after all those years, her story has taken on the aspect of a mirage, a drama somehow of her own making. What she had not expected, though, was that in sharing her story, its real meaning would emerge.

Acknowledgements

My thanks to Jan Woolf for her expert and kind editing, for dusting the book with great care and making several discerning suggestions, and my warmest thanks to Patricia Taylor for her support, patience and generosity in reading the numerous drafts I inflicted on her along the months. Her clear mind was a great help when I was losing my focus.

BOOKS

O is a symbol of the world, of oneness and unity; this eye represents knowledge and insight. We publish titles on general spirituality and living a spiritual life. We aim to inform and help you on your own journey in this life.

Visit our website: http://www.o-books.com

Find us on Facebook:
https://www.facebook.com/OBooks

Follow us on Twitter: @obooks